D0975590

Angels in
Disguise

Angels in Disguise

WHEN GOD SENDS ANIMALS TO COMFORT US

EDITED BY PHYLLIS HOBE

Guideposts
New York, New York

Angels in Disguise

ISBN-13:978-0-8249-4782-8

Published by Guideposts
16 East 34th Street
New York, New York 10016
Guideposts.org

Distributed by Ideals Publications, a division of Guideposts
2636 Elm Hill Pike, Suite 120
Nashville, Tennessee 37214

Guideposts and *Ideals* are registered trademarks of Guideposts.

Acknowledgments

Every attempt has been made to credit the sources of copyrighted material used in this book. If any such acknowledgment has been inadvertently omitted or miscredited, receipt of such information would be appreciated.

"Kimberly's Best Friend" by Brad Steiger is from *Cat Caught My Heart* by Michael Capuzzo and Teresa Banik Capuzzo. Copyright © 1999 by Michael Capuzzo and Teresa Banik Capuzzo. Published by Bantam Books. Used by permission of the author.

"Weela, a Community Hero" is from *It Takes a Dog to Raise a Village* by Ruth Gordon. Copyright © by Ruth Gordon. Published by Willow Creek Press.

All other stories are reprinted by permission of the authors.

Scripture quotations marked (KJV) are taken from *The King James Version of the Bible*.

Scripture quotations marked (NIV) are taken from *The Holy Bible, New International Version*. Copyright © 1973, 1978, 1984 International Bible Society. Used by permission of Zondervan Bible Publishers.

Library of Congress Cataloging-in-Publication Data

Angels in disguise : when God sends animals to comfort us / edited by Phyllis Hobe.
    p. cm.
  ISBN 978-0-8249-4782-8
  1. Animals—Religious aspects—Christianity—Anecdotes. I. Hobe, Phyllis.
  BV4596.A54A46 2009
  242—dc22

                                    2009011506

Cover design by Robin Bilardello
Cover photograph by Getty Images
Interior design by Gretchen Schuler-Dandridge
Typeset by Nancy Tardi

Printed and bound in the United States of America

10 9 8 7 6 5 4 3

Contents

Angels in
Disguise

LIFE-CHANGING MOMENTS

Be strong and of a good courage,
fear not, nor be afraid....

DEUTERONOMY 31:6 (KJV)

The Peacekeeper

GLORIA CASSITY STARGEL

THE DAY OUR YOUNGER son Rick left home for the Marine Corps was a heart-wrenching one for me. Beside the fact that I just hate good-byes, this was my "baby" going off to become a fighting man. I couldn't help worrying that military training would destroy Rick's loving, compassionate spirit. *Dear Lord, make him tough, if necessary. But, please, Lord*, I prayed, *keep him tender*. Now who but a mother would make a request like that?

Rick endured the rigors of basic training and Officer Candidate School. Then, after advanced instruction, he was assigned to the Marine Corps Air Station in Cherry Point, North Carolina. There—seeking a little off-duty peace and quiet of his own—he rented a small house out in the country. Always athletic, he looked forward to the solitude of his daily six-mile run along picturesque fields and meadows.

A problem developed, though. It seems that on each farm there were several large dogs. They didn't take too kindly to this strange intruder racing through their territories. Every day, by the time Rick made it back to his house, he was tripping over a whole pack of yelping dogs, most of them snarling at his heels. It was not the tranquil time he had envisioned. Hoping to discourage the attackers, he tried kicking, swinging a stick, yelling. Nothing worked.

One day, Rick phoned home. "Mother," he began, "you know those dogs that have been making my life miserable? Well, I remembered you taught us that 'kindness always pays.' So I decided to give it a try."

"What did you do?" I asked.

"Yesterday, as I ran," he said, "when my patience had been pushed to the limit, I just stopped in my tracks, whirled around to face them, stooped down on one knee, and talked to them in my best 'pet-talk' voice. And you know what?" Rick's voice was smiling now. "Those dogs started wagging their tails and kissing me on the face, each trying to get closer than the other."

"What happened today when you ran?" I wanted to know.

"You wouldn't believe the difference," Rick said. "It was so peaceful! Passing one farm after the other, the whole crowd fell in and ran as usual. But this time they ran *with* me—not against me. I must have looked like the Pied Piper by the time we got back to my house." I smiled into the phone, picturing my young, still-sensitive son. For Rick had solved his problem. And God had answered a mother's prayer.

The Eagle's Answer

BROOKE MARTINI

*O*UR SUMMER ESCAPE AND means of relaxation had always been the lake that we live on. We used the lake for all seasons: swimming in the summer, fishing in the spring and fall, and ice skating in the winter.

On a lazy summer day not too long ago, my mom and I discussed facts and feelings about the divorce she and my dad were going through. Living in the situation was exhausting. I would simply try to forget that it even existed, because I was over twenty-one and trying to begin a life of my own. The conversation was exasperating. We were asking questions that neither one of us could answer.

Questions such as "How long can this go on?" "Am I doing the right thing?" "Why does it have to be this way?"

I didn't want to discuss the matter any further and we both fell silent. A few minutes later, as we were floating in the water on a couple of air mattresses, we saw a big, beautiful eagle soar over our house, circling us on the lake. It stayed in sight a minute or two before disappearing back over our house. It never flapped its wings. It never made a sound.

My mom and I were awestruck. One of my mom's favorite verses is Isaiah 40:31 (NIV): "Those who wait upon the Lord will renew their strength. They will soar on wings like eagles; they will run and not grow weary, they will walk and not be faint."

God spoke to us that day through one of His beautiful creations. We immediately knew that although we still had so many questions, we had to wait for the answers to come in His time. For when we have persevered, the difficulty we once knew will be gone and we will gain strength.

It has been almost a year and the trying family situation we lived in seems to be coming to a close. Some of our questions remain unanswered, but friends around us—who don't know our eagle story—have told us that when the difficulty is finally over, we will soar. We often think of that eagle and are continually reminded to wait for God's timing, not our own. How awesome is our Creator!

Black Magic

DIANE M. CIARLONI

I WAS THE ONLY ONE in my family with "That Ol' Black Magic" passion for horses. Actually, I was the only one in my family with a passion for animals. My parents assumed the "Okay, you may have them if you'll care for them, and if we can afford to feed them" attitude. My brother certainly didn't dislike them but, overall, he was one of the "ho-hum" variety. And my sister . . . well, let's just say we were different.

I had one horse, a beautiful Tennessee Walker named Bob. A few days following my fourteenth birthday, a neighboring friend told me about a black mare.

"She's really pretty," he said, "but she's wild. She's been running on about forty acres with a dozen or so mules. The guy who owns the land told me she's been there at least three or four years, which is why she's so wild. He also told me her owner hasn't paid rent for over eighteen months."

There was a point to his story, and I knew he hadn't made it yet. I was familiar with all of Robert's patterns. He was seventeen, with a flair for the dramatic. I always thought he used it to draw attention away from the birth defect that burdened him with a left arm that was nothing more than an abbreviated, wilted-looking appendage.

So I waited.

"Anyway, Mr. Burns—he's the one who owns the place—told me we can have her if we can catch her."

"What do you mean 'have her'?" I queried.

He shook his head. "I mean just what I said. We can have her. Free. For nothing. All we need to do is catch her."

"And just how wild is she?" I asked.

He grinned and then he laughed. "Pretty darned wild. Wanna' go look at her?"

"How are we going to look at her if she's running

wild on forty acres?" I countered. I knew there would be an answer.

"Because every evening around five thirty Mr. Burns throws out some hay and a little grain in a corner that's nearest his house. The mare and the mules go up to eat."

I got up from my chair. That was all he needed to signal a "yes" on my part.

I knew where the Burns' place was located, no more than three or four miles from my parents' farm. Most of it was overgrown. I'd noticed a few mules inside the barbed wire fencing but had never caught sight of a black mare.

The trip was short and, just as we drove down the rocky drive leading to the old house, Mr. Burns was walking back to the barn with a couple of empty buckets.

I sat in Robert's truck with the window down, looking. Sure enough, just as he said, there was a beautiful black mare standing in the middle of the mules. At least, she would be beautiful with some loving attention and care. As things were, her long mane and tail were matted with burrs. Her forelock was no better, standing straight out from her forehead in a compact burr column, making her look like a ragamuffin unicorn. Her feet were grown out to the point of being inhumane and, even from a distance, I could see that one eye was infected.

"Her eye," I said. "The right one is infected. She probably poked a thistle in it."

"Just how would you propose to catch her?" I continued. "We sure couldn't walk up to her and slip on a halter and lead rope, especially if she stays bunched inside those mules. Do you know how hard those things kick? And they'll run right over you if they can't get in a good kick."

He chuckled. "Yeah, I know that, but here's what I was thinking. It might sound a little complicated, so listen."

I frowned at him, resenting the tone that made me sound less than intelligent.

"He's already feeding them in a corner. We come over here the night before and string a second set of wire so it reaches from one side of the corner to the other to make a triangle."

I rolled my eyes skyward. I already knew where he was headed, but I let him go on and assume the dramatic role of mastermind. It cost me nothing, and it made him feel good.

"The next day they go into the triangle to eat. We

ride over and let our horses distract them. Finally, we jump in and each of us grabs a strand of the loose wire, beats it to the opposite corner, and attaches it loosely so you can undo it in a hurry."

Robert paused. He seemed out of breath, as if experiencing the entire procedure he'd just described. "I get inside the enclosure and shoo out the mules, one by one, toward you. You undo the wire and let them go through. Then you rehook the wire until the next one comes."

I looked at him in disbelief. "And you really and truly think this will work?" I asked in dismay. "What happens when about six of those mules—and maybe even the mare herself—charge toward me at once? Surely you don't think a couple of pieces of wire will stop those stubborn-headed things. Who's gonna' scrape me up after they flatten me on the ground? I'll be stuck down there for the rest of my life and, because I'm only fourteen, that will be a darned long time. And how do you intend to keep the mare from going out the same opening? And—"

"Look," he interrupted, in an irritated tone. "This is a free horse. Free! She's not a spring chicken but she's still plenty young enough to have a baby or two, and how many times have you said that's what you've always wanted?

"Sure, it'll take a lot of patience and plenty of work, but I guarantee you we'll get her."

A new thought suddenly found its way across my brainwaves. Yes, I definitely wanted this mare and, yes, I definitely would like to breed her. *But*, I thought, *I had someone who was enough of a friend to help me do this crazy thing.*

I smiled and shook my head in the affirmative. We got out of the truck and greeted Mr. Burns, filling him in on our plan. He was as skeptical as I'd been but, as far as he was concerned, it was our lives and limbs at risk. He did, however, make us promise to tell our parents and, further, make them promise not to sue him should anything happen to us. We agreed.

As soon as we faced nothing but green lights, owning the mare became a reality. I pictured her in our barn, named her Black Magic for her coat and because it would be sheer magic when (not if) we caught her. I was even thinking about a chocolate-colored stallion named Soldier, who belonged to Mr. Diggs, another neighbor. Soldier would be a perfect breeder for Black Magic, who was as good as mine, although we hadn't made the first move toward capturing her.

I told my parents the entire story. They assumed

their "As long as you take care of her, etc." stance, but I knew they were saying it because they didn't think there was even a remote chance we'd succeed.

The plan was in place and we began executing it the following evening. The wire was twisted around the gnarled, crusty tree branches that served as fence posts. We used smooth wire instead of barbed to protect my hands because I would be the one executing that part of the scheme.

We were time-synced with Mr. Burns for the next afternoon. That night, I went to bed and, naturally, couldn't sleep.

The sun finally came up. The day passed and we saddled our horses for the ride to Mr. Burns. He was just dumping the feed when we dismounted and tied up to the fence. Robert was right. The mules as well as the mare immediately turned their attention to the newcomers. The plan was already succeeding!

We began working, and we worked and we worked and . . . my hands, even with gloves, looked and felt mangled. We both fell dozens of times, skinning elbows and ripping the knees of our jeans. We were covered with dirt and stickers. Tiny rocks lodged in our shoes. To this day, I still wonder how Robert held up his end of the plan with only one arm.

Darkness fell and we were down to three mules and Black Magic. Mr. Burns switched on all five of his big outside floodlights. We sat down on the ground to confer. The main question was: Should we continue or should we hold off until tomorrow?

"If we leave," said Robert, "the other mules will come back and irritate the mare and the mules who're still in the pen. I'm afraid she will hurt herself trying to get out."

"Fine," I rebutted. "If we get the other three mules out tonight, what will we do with the mare? We sure can't load her up in a trailer and take her home because she's about as wild as a March hare. She needs to stay here and be tamed down some. But if we leave her, the same thing will happen that you've already described."

Robert didn't say anything.

I charged into the silence, sarcastically, "Seems to me this part of the plan isn't quite jelled."

"Maybe not," he answered, "but I know there's a solution."

Maybe, but what was it?

It was Mr. Burns who solved the knotty problem. He

was pointing behind him as he walked over to us. "That corral over there is old, but it's sound and sturdy," he said. "It would put quite a bit of distance between the mare and the mules, and I don't think she could break out of it or hurt herself."

"But how do we get her over there?" I asked.

"Doing the same thing you've already done," he responded. "String about three strands of wire from either side of the corner to the corral gate. That'll make a sort of alley. Then herd her over there. You'll need to be careful, but you've already done what I thought you'd never do! Besides, the worst that can happen is that she breaks out and gets loose around here. And, even if she did, she'd just go back to the mules."

It sounded good. We picked up the roll of wire and cutters but, just as we headed for our target area, Mr. Burns held up his hand. He obviously had another brainstorm.

"Wait," he commanded. "I have some hogwire in the barn. If you use that, it'll seem more like a solid wall." Gee, he was really getting into this. Again, we agreed.

Thirty minutes later the "walls" were up, but we needed more than two hours to get rid of the remaining mules. As soon as they were gone, we ran to the two posts attached to the hogwire. We clipped the barbed wire and kicked it out of the way. Black Magic, covered in lather and wild-eyed, whirled around and looked at the gaping opening. She was confused. We kept our voices calm and started shooing her toward the alleyway leading to the corral.

It was a frightening, rather torturous process for the first fifteen or twenty minutes. Then, like a bolt of lightning, Black Magic decided to break for the corral gate. As soon as she was in, Mr. Burns jumped into the gap with both arms stretched out to hold her in. In the meantime, we cut the wire and slammed the wooden gate shut.

No one could believe it. Black Magic was actually in the corral! Before total exhaustion claimed us, we hauled buckets of water and feed. Then we mounted our horses and rode back in the dark.

The following day began weeks and weeks of hard work. We did everything possible to gentle the mare. Soothing voices. Special treats. Hours of sitting calmly and silently outside her corral gate. More hours standing motionless inside the gate.

Nothing worked. She refused the treats. She bolted as soon as we took one small step in her direction. She'd been in the corral three weeks and, still, all we could see of her eyes were the whites. And she was losing weight at a nearly alarming rate. She munched only sparingly at the hay, and not even that if she could see anyone around.

"How could she get this wild in less than two years?" I asked Mr. Burns.

"Don't know," he answered. "I guess God created some animals to be wild, and others He created to be part of a person's life. The wild ones have a different spirit. I've seen folks try to force the first ones into the second group, and I can tell you the result is pitiful. You could call it broken. I hate to tell you this, but I think this mare belongs to the first group."

Somewhere, deep inside my soul, I think I heard the truth in Mr. Burns' voice, but I wasn't ready to give up. She had a name. She was no longer just the black mare. She was Black Magic. And she had a breeding to Soldier coming up and, in my heart's eye, I could already see her long-legged baby running like the wind across the pasture.

I just needed to work harder.

And I did work harder, and Black Magic refused to respond. There were moments—very fleeting moments— when I caught a different look in her eyes. It was the faintest of all possible hints that she would like to be a part of my life but, unlike me, she'd accepted that it wasn't meant to be. Now that I'm much, much older, I look back and smile.

I think of Black Magic and me like ill-fated, star-crossed lovers. The attraction was there, but it would be fatal. It was just a matter of who recognized it first. In this case, it was Black Magic.

I knew what had to be done. Black Magic's coat was dull. Her eyes were sadly lackluster. She was a different horse than the one we'd worked so hard to capture two months earlier. It was time to turn her loose and, somewhere inside my fourteen-year-old soul, I knew it was more than turning loose just one black horse. I knew it was also turning loose dreams and hopes. And although I didn't realize it then, it was also finding out that, sometimes, the best way to show love is to turn something or someone loose. And I also learned that sometimes it's better not to capture something in the first place.

The hogwire alleyway was still in place. I opened the corral gate and waited until Black Magic turned her head toward the opening. She eyed it. She stood still and then looked at me. She watched me and waited. All I did was nod my head. I still don't know how, but she knew what I was telling her. She didn't run. She just trotted down the alleyway and into the pasture where the mules had waited for her for the entire two months. She stopped once and looked back at me.

A kid can't possibly know what he or she is learning as life's equations fall into some sort of sequential order. And certainly no one ever knows what form the teachers will assume. In this case, it was a black mare with burrs in her mane and tail and outgrown feet. I learned about freedom and sacrifice. I learned about caring enough to let go, a lesson I carried with me each time I was faced with putting a beloved animal to sleep. I learned that sometimes people and animals enter our lives for only a short time, passing through the portals of our hearts just long enough to leave us with the results of an important lesson or the seeds of a life-changing idea.

Black Magic was a teacher. I never went to see her again. For whatever reason, it seemed that merely "visiting" her would break apart something very special. It was like a piece of that hogwire was keeping us attached to each other and, even though I'd learned about freedom, I didn't want to cut us apart forever.

I never did get a mare and I never did get a baby. But that was just as well because there was no room for them in the corner of my heart that was still occupied by the black mare and her chocolate-colored foal. Now, all these many, many years later, I can still feel the spell woven by that ol' Black Magic.

A Miracle Named Munchie

THIRZA PEEVEY

I MADE IT TO THE SHOWER and turned the water on full blast before I started crying. My roommates didn't need to know that I was crying. I didn't want to depress them.

I just didn't know what else to do for my friend Frances. I was totally at a loss and so were her doctors. Three months ago, she had the flu. She thought the cats must have been sleeping on her feet while she was sick, but the tingly, painful sensation didn't go away. Instead it began creeping up her legs. It moved on to her hands and arms. It kept steadily creeping upward.

Her doctors were perplexed at first, but after a spinal tap they offered up the diagnosis of Guillain-Barré syndrome. "It's a rare disease," they told me. "Actually we've never seen it before. We really can't do anything for her except give her painkillers. She doesn't have health insurance, so we are going to let you take her home and watch her. If the paralysis gets to her chest, she will die and there is nothing we can do. We wouldn't be able to do much even if she were here in the hospital. If she makes it to Monday, we will do another spinal tap and see if it is advancing or retreating."

Frances had made it to Monday, and in fact the paralysis had started reversing, so she refused the second spinal tap. That was when the real trial started. As the paralysis had moved forward, it had damaged and even killed many nerve cells. At least, that was the explanation offered at the time. As the paralysis reversed, the nerve cells started to heal and regenerate. That was when the severe pain began. Most of the time, the painkillers barely dulled the pain. She sat in her bed and shook with the intensity of it and bit her lip until it bled to keep from screaming. She said she felt as if her arms and legs were on fire. Her feet felt as if the bones were coming through the skin. Lord only knows what mixed-up messages her brain was getting from the damaged nerve cells.

Frances' husband was starting a new business and couldn't be in both places at once, so I tried to help every way I could. I came every night after work and took care of her seven cats, three dogs, one rabbit and one pony. I changed her bed and got her something to eat. I tidied the house and vacuumed. I did the laundry and the dishes. I set out drinks, snacks and medicine for the next day and made sure she had the TV remote and things to read, because she was trapped in bed and couldn't walk. But I couldn't stop the soul-destroying pain. Nothing touched it. So every night I took care of her needs and tucked her into bed and then I went home and stood in the shower and cried.

The months passed and the pain continued. By sheer grit, Frances was regaining the use of her arms and legs. True to her cantankerous nature, she began crawling around the house on her hands and knees to do housework. Some days I arrived to find her pants soaked in blood around the knees from crawling until her knees blistered and the blisters broke. That made it better somehow for her because she didn't feel as helpless, but it made me feel terrible. Time and time again we squabbled over staying in bed so her body could heal. Actually, I squabbled. She looked away and refused to listen.

Within a few weeks, Frances discovered that one leg was strong enough to support her. The other could support her weight from the knee up, but the foot and lower leg were too weak. She overcame this difficulty by taking a lightweight side chair and using it as a peg leg. She would kneel on the chair with the weak leg while she swung the strong one forward. Then, standing on the strong leg, she pulled the chair and the weak leg forward. In this unorthodox fashion she began getting around the house to dust, cook and vacuum. Soon she was taking care of everything but the laundry and the cat pans. That made her feel a little less helpless and bored, but the crushing pain and the feeling of being trapped remained. We still didn't know if it was ever going to get better.

Spring arrived, and with it, her favorite time of year. She was walking now, but her left leg was not much bigger around than the bone itself. All of the muscle had wasted away. Her balance was severely affected by the lack of strength on that side and she couldn't trust herself on uneven ground. She was trapped indoors and could only watch spring unfold through the window. I think that was almost harder for her than all the rest of the indignities of being sick. So far, her orneriness had kept her going, but I wondered how long she could cope with being unable to do the things she loved. Then one weekend, she pounced.

As I came in to the house, she ordered me, "Go get Munchie. Harness her up and put her to the work cart. Meet me outside the garage in half an hour." I was a bit startled, to say the least. Munchie was her little white Welsh pony. Purchased for her daughter fifteen years before, Farnley Keepsake had proved to be a bit too much pony for a child. She had repeatedly bucked the child off and then galloped away with her tail flipped over her back. Something about her ornery nature had appealed to Frances, however, and the two had bonded. Frances broke the pony to drive a cart. Christened Munchkin or Munchie, she became a local star at carriage-driving shows. Soon the interior walls of both garages were covered with ribbons that Frances and Munchie had won. I had shown against Munchie, however, and I knew what a handful that pony could be. There was no way Frances could drive the pony in her current condition, even in an indoor arena, and I told her so.

"Listen," Frances replied, "I have been driving that pony over the same route every day for fifteen years. She knows the route. She knows to look both ways before pulling out into traffic. She knows to wait while I open the gate to the practice field. She can drive our route without me. Get the pony, I'm going driving."

I suppose I could have said no. In Frances' current condition she couldn't have done much about it, but something told me it would break her spirit if I did. I went and got the pony. *Besides*, I thought to myself as I groomed the pony and harnessed her, *I'll be there to help if anything goes wrong.* When I finished preparing the pony, I helped Frances out the door and supported her as she sat on the seat and pivoted into the cart. I started to step into the cart myself, but she picked up the whip and shook it at me.

"Now you go away," she said. "I'll be back in an hour and I'll need you to help me out of the cart and put the pony away."

Well, what else was I going to do? I let her go. I watched the pony trot to the end of the lane and wait for traffic to clear. Then she turned left into the road, carefully leaving enough room for the cart to clear the farm signboard so that the wheels wouldn't catch. I went in the house and started my chores, frantically checking the windows every few minutes and listening for the sounds of hooves on the road. An hour later I was relieved to hear slow clip-clopping as Munchie walked in the driveway. I hurried downstairs to help Frances out of the cart and put away the pony.

Frances was radiant. "I got to forget, just for a little while, about the pain and about being sick. For a little while I got to be alone and not have anyone fussing over me. I got to just be me. But now my feet are freezing—get me in the house, please."

Ever patient, Munchie stood quietly outside the garage until I had Frances settled in a chair upstairs. Then I came downstairs, unhooked Munchie, and put the harness away. I gave her a good brushing and took her to the barn. "You are some pony, old girl," I whispered into her tiny white ears. "I think you may have found a way to give us all hope."

A few weeks later, Munchie showed me that she really did know how to drive herself, and I didn't need to worry about them in traffic. I heard Munchie coming in the driveway and went out to meet her as usual. Frances wasn't in the cart. "Where did you leave Mom, old girl?" I asked her. I was just about to get in the cart and go looking when I saw Frances jogging down the driveway. When she caught her breath, she told me what had happened.

"When I closed the gate at Hathaway's, I tripped and stumbled against the cart. Munchie thought I'd gotten in and started up the hill. I tried to catch her, but I wasn't quick enough. She paused at the top of the hill, looked both ways, and turned onto the right side of the road. She walked the first few paces, as I'd taught her, and then broke into a trot just as if I was in the carriage. I almost caught her, but I was a split second too slow. At the end of the street, she stopped for the stop sign and waited for traffic to clear. As heavy as traffic is on Caves Road, I almost caught up to her again, but she got a break in the traffic and turned right toward home, being careful to leave enough clearance so the hub wouldn't catch the stop sign. She stayed on the right side near the shoulder, trotted all the way to our lane, and then turned right into the driveway, again leaving clearance for the signboard. She came right to the garage door and stopped for me to get out."

"I know," I replied. "She couldn't understand where you were. She kept looking around, trying to find you."

After that, I never worried about them being out alone together. Munchie really could drive herself and, thanks to that little incident, I knew that Frances was now strong enough to walk home if need be. Frances drove her almost every day and began feeling more like herself and less like a patient. Walking to and from the cart and opening the gate at Hathaway's all forced her to walk independently and built strength back in her legs. Holding the reins forced her to use her hands and arms and rebuilt strength there too. Most of all, it lifted her spirits.

Before long, Frances could get the pony from the barn by herself and wasn't dependent on me or my schedule anymore. Through the summer she grew stronger and stronger. Within a year of the onset of the illness, she was nearly back to normal, except for one cold foot.

I suppose that she would have mended without the pony, but I still believe the turning point came when Munchie gave her something to look forward to each day. That was when Frances began to believe she would make it. And she did.

The Day the Cows Could Count

KATHRYN MAYS as told to
LONNIE HULL DuPONT

I GREW UP ON A small dairy farm in northern Michigan. We had about fifty head of cattle at any given time, and it was my chore in the morning to help my father milk them before he left for his work as a high-school teacher. My brothers and sisters joined in the milking again after we came home from school. In my sixteenth year, something happened on the farm that not only convinced me that God was looking out for me but also that God has a sense of humor.

I loved the farm, and I loved the ritual of milking. I was the oldest of five children, but this early morning chore was something I did alone with my father, whom I have always adored. Each morning the cows would wait patiently outside the barn for the milking. Dad and I would usher them inside, six at a time, milk them and then usher them back out the other side of the barn through a different door. As we hooked them up to the milking equipment, I would think about my day and my life. It was usually dark and often cold—sometimes extremely cold—but the cows' steaming breath and their passive trust always warmed me up. It was a fine way to start a day.

Cows must be milked twice a day, no matter what. If they aren't milked, they can get mastitis, a not uncommon infection, for which they need antibiotics. This renders a cow's milk unusable until she heals up. Even when a cow is sick, however, she has to be milked, and that milk cannot be consumed or sold. It must be poured out.

One time I had neglected to separate the mastitis milk from the rest of the herd's daily take. That evening, my father made me pour the entire day's milking down a drain in the barn floor by myself. None of that day's milk from any of our cows could be sold. I cried the entire time I poured. Dad wasn't unkind; he simply wanted me never again to forget this important—and expensive—detail. And I never did forget.

One Sunday when I was sixteen, my family was away for the day. I don't remember why I was alone, but night milking needed to be done, and I'd have to do it by myself. Five cows had mastitis and were on antibiotics. Each cow had a number attached to her ear, and Dad had given me a list of the five infected cows' numbers. I would need to pour out the milk from those cows. The best way to do all this was to separate the infected cows from the rest of the herd and then milk everybody.

At low light, I headed for the barn. There in a small corral were the fifty cows, all crowded together, all waiting for me to milk them. Now cows aren't like horses. They're big and passive and not exactly high-energy, so they aren't the easiest creatures to lead. Getting five specific cows out of this herd was going to be difficult.

First I'd have to weave in between them and read their numbers to find the right five cows. Then I'd need to throw on a lead rope or prod them somehow to get each one of them out of there and herded into another pen without the other cows getting out too. And, as I say, cows aren't horses—they don't automatically move aside. They're very curious and, consequently, they may actually get in the way and become obstacles. Or they may just decide to follow an infected cow out of the corral. Then I'd have to get the infected cow into the other pen and the healthy cow back into the corral, keeping the rest of the herd from spilling out—by myself!

So although separating the five ailing cows from the rest wouldn't be an impossible task, it wasn't going to be an easy one. Or short. Memories of pouring milk down the drain still smarted. I didn't want to mess this up.

I opened the gate and entered the corral. The cows—as cows are wont to do—turned as a group and stared at me. I suddenly wished my siblings were there to help.

It occurred to me that God cares about all the details of our lives—of my life. Perhaps this was a time to enlist the Lord's help. So while I held the list of numbers in one hand, I raised my other hand in the air—it seemed appropriate to do that. Then, with all the faith of a child, I spoke in a loud voice toward the heavens: "In the name of the Lord Jesus Christ, would the following cows please step forward? Numbers two, eleven, seventeen, thirty-two and forty-nine."

I don't know why I said that or even why I said it that way. I felt pretty silly and was glad no one else was around. But as soon as I finished speaking, I heard a rustling noise from the back of the corral.

You know what happened, of course. Cows numbered two, eleven, seventeen, thirty-two and forty-nine wriggled their way through the herd and came forward. And other cows actually stepped aside for them. I was reminded of the parting of the Red Sea. I picked up my jaw from the ground, opened the gate, herded each of the five into the other pen and then locked the rest of the amazingly cooperative herd back up to prepare to milk. Separating the sick cows probably took me all of two minutes, and milking that early evening took no more time than usual.

I didn't tell my folks about it that night. In fact, I usually never tell this story. Who would believe it? It's the only time something like that has ever happened in my life. But I never forgot it, and I've always appreciated it.

As I said, I like to think God has a sense of humor—we're made in his image, after all. It's true that on that day God smiled on me and made the work of this young laborer a little easier. But when he used a herd of dairy cows as his agents, I like to imagine that he winked too.

GIFTS
FROM GOD

*"Please accept the present that was
brought to you, for God has been
gracious to me and I have all I need"....*

GENESIS 33:11 (NIV)

How Jellybean Went to Kansas

DIANE M. CIARLONI

I COULD FEEL MY heartstrings stretch to near breaking every time I watched Kansas. He was so timid with people and with other animals. So shy he could hardly raise his eyes to meet someone else's gaze.

Kansas was just a "regular" cat. Absolutely nothing about him was physically special. He was short-legged and stocky, riding low to the ground. The shape of his head was on the square side, giving him the appearance of a miniature bobcat. He was gray striped. That's it. Just gray striped. No white. Nothing stood out. He did have one unique characteristic, but few people other than I were ever privileged to see it because it was his belly. Instead of being gray, it was a very soft fawn color with black spots that even the vet found extremely unusual.

Kansas hung around for more than two months before approaching me, but when he did make up his mind, he seemed determined to do everything at once. I was sitting outside on a bench when he suddenly burst from the bushes and landed in my lap. He plopped down and graced me with a lapful of purr. That was it. I'd coaxed and coaxed, but the timid little thing needed time to work up his courage.

Kansas certainly must have been overwhelmed when he first came into the house. There were other cats as well as dogs, birds and a large black lop bunny named Jellybean. It was enough to daunt even a self-confident cat, which Kansas definitely was not. I thought he would socialize and become braver with time, but he didn't. The extent of his comfortable world was my lap. Everything else was scary.

It was so easy to watch Kansas and mentally change him into the shiest first-grader on the playground. Remember? Maybe it was even you. Standing with hands behind back, tucked away from the other kids but close enough to hear them laughing and see them running and playing. Everything about them seemed so wonderful. You imagined taking that first step and joining them, but somehow the step never went beyond a thought. It didn't matter that every fiber of your being wanted to join that group. Your feet were tied to the ground and you just couldn't move. That's the way it was with Kansas.

Many, many times I looked on as the dogs played tug-of-war with a strip of rawhide. Kansas watched, inching backward into a corner when their play-growling became too loud. I watched him as the other cats pounced on a ball with a bell in it or courageously "killed" a fur mouse. He seemed to accept the fact that he would never be a part of all their activity. There were times when I asked myself if, perhaps, he would have been better off outside and on his own. I could watch his shy misery only so long before inviting him into my lap. I knew that was probably the worst thing I could do, but I couldn't help myself.

The fact that the other cats strongly discouraged Kansas' participation in their games didn't help the situation. At times he made half-hearted attempts to be "one of the guys," but he was inevitably rebuffed with slaps or hisses. When that happened, he backed quickly out of the limelight and looked for me. Oh, how my heart ached for the little gray cat! Then, just when I was standing on the brink of despair, Jellybean decided to take things into her own paws.

Jellybean was, in a word, sweet. There was nothing pushy about the big, velvetlike, black lop, but being sweet did not mean she was retiring. It simply meant she was persistent in a pleasing manner and, further, it meant she was difficult to resist. What developed between Kansas and Jellybean was truly amazing.

One day, while I was working at my computer, my peripheral vision caught sight of Jellybean hopping to Kansas, who, as usual, sat on the sidelines of what appeared to be the cat-and-dog Olympics. She reached his side, turned around and sat down next to him. As a matter of fact, she was very close to him—as in squashed against his plain, gray fur. Kansas looked down at the rabbit but offered no resistance to what was plainly an overture of some kind. Neither did he try to run away, which, in itself, was rather odd.

Jellybean sat very quietly for five minutes or less. Then she reached over and delivered a couple of bunny kisses before returning to her house. As I said, it was odd behavior and, somehow, I knew more would follow.

That initial contact between Kansas and Jellybean was followed by several more. Sometimes the gray cat and the black bunny paired up seven or eight times during the course of a day. I was fascinated with what was happening, but when I tried to tell friends, no one believed me. Jellybean was actually leading Kansas one, or maybe two steps closer each day to the other animals. She stayed by his side and, with her there, he never noticed the possibility of what he perceived as danger. Instead, the solid warmth of Jellybean's presence was forming the cornerstone of his newly developing confidence.

Jellybean had her own ball, one of those little plastic things with a tiny bell inside. One of her games was to hook her beaverlike teeth into the ball and toss it with a flip of her neck. Weakly powered by her scant force, it barely "sailed" more than three or four inches, but on a really good effort, it would roll across the carpet until Jellybean hopped over and stopped its forward motion. Once the rabbit had coaxed Kansas more than halfway across the floor of my office, she began playing ball with him. It didn't take long for Kansas to get the hang of things. Before many practice sessions passed, he and Jellybean were conducting their games at a fever-pitch intensity. Then, after more than two months of Jellybean's coaxing and training, it happened.

It was midafternoon and everyone was awakening from naps. That meant new energy reserves available for play. The dogs started off slowly, grabbing rawhide chew toys and anchoring them between their front paws for easier destruction. The cats were prowling, trying to decide what to do. Jellybean found her ball, lowered her black head, and butted it to Kansas. The bell inside its frame jingled a merry tune as it headed toward the gray cat. But just before the ball reached him, Doso, a very large Maine Coon, stepped in front of it. He stopped its progress by placing one big, flat, white paw on top of it. When he knew the ball was secure, he turned his head toward Kansas. I could see the gray cat falter. I could almost feel his shyness returning. *Oh please, Kans*, I thought. *Jellybean has worked so hard, buddy. Don't let her down.*

I was almost certain I saw Kansas shift his weight and sit up straighter and taller. He relaxed, and just as he did, Doso swiped his paw across the carpet and sent the ball rolling toward Kansas. Do cats smile? How about rabbits? I certainly think they do. As a matter of fact, I would probably take an oath that I saw smiles playing across the faces of Kansas and Jellybean as the gray tabby leaped on the ball and took off around the room with the Coon in hot pursuit. That was the day Kansas joined, and he stayed joined from there on.

Did Kansas leave Jellybean behind once he fell into

step with the guys? No, he did not. They still enjoyed their special times with each other on four or five occasions each week. The Bible tells us, "A faithful friend is a strong defense: and he who has found such a one has found a treasure." That was, indeed, Jellybean. She was Kansas' defense for as long as he needed her. She never wavered. She was a treasure who opened his eyes to the many possibilities of the wonderful world around him.

Jellybean and Kansas are both gone, but they didn't leave without teaching me a valuable lesson. They showed me how friendship focuses, friend to friend. They showed me how one friend can serve another without feeling a need to say, "Goodness! Look at what I'm doing for you." They showed me that one of the greatest joys of friendship is quietly helping a friend to move into bigger, broader spaces without fear of losing him. Plainly and simply speaking, they offered up a definition of friendship, and, I will always thank them for showing me the true meaning of something I once read, something that said, "It is not what you give your friend, but what you are willing to give him, that determines the quality of friendship."

For Such a Time As This

GLORIA CASSITY STARGEL

SHE CAME TO US with fear and trembling. She left with our hearts. Her name was Misty Dawn.

But wait, I'm getting ahead of my story.

It was on a blustery winter's night that I answered the doorbell's ring to find young Joey Lancaster and his Mom. Joey was holding a huge bundle of long silver fur. From that bundle shone two great big yellow-green eyes on an adorable, pug-nosed face. And draped under Joey's arm was a long, silver plumelike tail. "That's the prettiest cat I ever saw," I said as I ushered them in from the cold.

This was to be a get-acquainted meeting. Joey had proven allergic to cats and needed to find a home for nine-month-old Misty. Being a cat person myself, I agreed to let her stay the weekend—"on trial."

I had no way of knowing that we would need her even more than she needed us. Misty wasn't sure she wanted us, either, and obviously was not happy among strangers in a new environment. She crouched behind furniture or stalked the perimeters of the house, seeking escape.

The next day was no better. I phoned the veterinarian for advice.

"I wouldn't adopt a full-grown cat," he said. "They don't easily transfer their affection." And, truth be told, I really wanted a kitten. On top of that, both our sons, though away at college, urged me to wait for a kitten.

I phoned Joey. "I'm afraid it's not going to work," I said.

He sounded disappointed. "Would you mind just keeping her a few more days until I can find her a home?" he asked.

"Sure, I can do that."

A week later, our son Randy called from school. "Mother, do you still have Misty?"

"Yes."

"Well, I've been thinking," he said, "maybe we ought to keep her."

"I've been thinking the same thing," I responded.

Rick, his brother, wholeheartedly agreed, and before long, with lots of tender, loving care, Misty knew she had found a home. She proved to be the most gentle of creatures, with the sweetest personality. Within days, however, it became evident that the time had come for her to be spayed. The afternoon when my husband Joe and I picked her up at the veterinarian's office following her surgery, we had just left our physician's office where we had learned that Joe himself required immediate surgery. The three of us were about to embark on a journey none of us wanted to take.

Thus began a four-year battle against a virulent strain of cancer—a fierce battle for Joe's life. We were swept along in a raging river, its waters wiping out all solid ground. During those first days and weeks, Misty was the one I turned to for solace. She was there when I cried bitter tears. And when I prayed fervent prayers. All during the year of debilitating treatments, Misty quietly and patiently provided a loving presence. When Joe became depressed and pulled away from close emotional contact, Misty's relaxed purr while she curled up in my lap provided comfort.

The following year, as a result of my praying and Joe's urging, I found myself back in college, a first-quarter sophomore after an absence of twenty-seven years! I recall how difficult that first quarter was. Just trying to read the next day's psychology lesson put me to sleep. It was Misty who kept me company while I studied late into the night.

By the time I received my degree from Brenau, I believed God was healing Joe. Further, I believed He wanted me to write about our experience. So Misty and I began work on my book, *The Healing; One Family's Victorious Struggle with Cancer*. It took four years—four years with Misty curled up in the top out-basket on the corner of my desk.

Not all was work, however. Being photogenic, Misty appeared in some rather interesting publications. *Modern Romance*, for instance! In our living room sits a life-sized white ceramic cat. Misty evidently felt some kinship and often visited with it. I managed to get a photo of them side-by-side in the same exact pose, standing regally with tails wrapped gracefully around front paws. You can hardly tell which is the live cat. The magazine featured that picture of Misty in their Pet column.

Another photo op came one night during a presidential debate. I was relaxing in the green recliner, with

Misty curled up behind my head. As the hour grew late and the debate grew boring, I stood up to go to bed. By now Misty was in a deep sleep, spread-eagled on top of the headrest. A picture of her in that caring-for-nothing position appeared in our local newspaper under the title "Debate? What Debate?"

Misty took part in our family celebrations too. Best of all, Joe was set free from cancer. Rick married and we gained a lovely daughter-in-law. Then Tyndale House published our book—and there, on the back cover, is Misty in the forefront of our family photo. For nineteen precious years, Misty was family. Nineteen years of our daily brushing sessions while we "talked it over." Nineteen years of trials, of triumphs.

But, as time will do, it took its toll. One night, while Misty and I sat on the couch watching television, she suddenly rolled off onto the floor, shaking violently. Her eyes mirrored terror—as did my own.

I fell to my knees and tried to calm her little body. "God," I cried out, "please help Misty!" Slowly, the seizure subsided, leaving both of us weak—and frightened.

It proved to be the first of several such episodes. Each time, I cried and prayed. And each time she grew weaker. I think she hung on because she didn't want to leave me, and I guess I was selfish. I just couldn't give her up. Then arthritis took over and robbed her of her dignity. Finally, when I saw that every moment was painful for her—that she could no longer even groom herself when she had always been so fastidious—I knew the time had come. I would have to let her go. Her doctor of all those years offered to come to our house rather than put her through the trauma of going to his office. All that afternoon, I sat and held her. I thought back to everything Misty and our family had been through together, especially facing Joe's illness. *Surely God sent you to us for such a time as this.* I told her how much I loved her, how beautiful she was, and what a fine family member she made. "I'll never forget you, Misty."

When the kind doctor left, Joe brought in the little wooden coffin a friend had made. He had even etched her name on top. We placed Misty there on the pillow I had covered in gold satin, tucked her blanket around her, and put in two of her favorite toys. I could go no further. While Joe conducted the burial in the woods behind our house, I sat down at the kitchen table and, with tears flowing, wrote this tribute:

Misty Dawn—Silver-tipped Persian
1972–1991
Pet, Companion, Friend.
She asked for little.
She gave her all.

                                 The Stargels

At Peace

MARY M. ALWARD

EARLY LAST SPRING my husband and I decided we needed to get away from it all. We wanted to go somewhere where there were no computers, no telephones and few people. We wanted to share a wilderness experience.

While scouring travel brochures, I came across The Homestead, a cabin resort in Ontario's Haliburton Highlands. It promised boating, fishing, solitude and a variety of spectacular nature experiences, depending on what time of year you visited. Immediately we made a reservation for the first week of June—off-season. Most people wouldn't start holidays until their children were out of school for the summer.

We left early on a Saturday morning and drove east through the congested heart of Toronto. From there, we took Highway 427 to Highway 11. Six hours after leaving southern Ontario, we pulled into the driveway of The Homestead. The place looked deserted.

Our hosts were a wonderful couple in their fifties. Their genuine hospitality gave us the feeling of being right at home. In addition, they had a friendly Alaskan malamute named Frosty who helped ease the ache of missing our own dog.

We arranged for a boat for the next day, unpacked the car, and settled into our cozy cabin. Early the next morning we were on the lake, which was a fantastic experience. The crystal water afforded us a great view of what lay in its depths. Large moss-covered rocks, algae and schools of fish made our spirits soar.

The scenery was breathtaking. Several islands dotted the lake. Pine trees seventy feet tall stretched to the sky. A wide variety of birds nested there.

We watched a hawk soar into the sky from an old rotten tree branch. He glided on the wind currents and then, with wings and feet outstretched, hit the water. In his sharp talons was a nice-sized fish. He flapped his wings, climbed into the sky, fish flapping, and disappeared.

It was a beautiful day. Cool enough for light jackets but just the right temperature. We anchored near the shore of one of the islands, and waited.

On shore, a doe came out of the woods and lifted her nose to sniff the air. Then she huffed a soft whoofing sound. The wind currents sent the sounds our way, but because she was upwind, she didn't smell us.

Out from the trees came two spotted fawns, twins. They walked behind their mother to the shore and drank deeply of the cold, clear lake water. After a few minutes, the doe lifted her head and looked directly at us. She gave a loud snort, flagged her tail and stamped her feet. The two fawns wheeled and leaped back into the forest, followed closely by their mother.

We stayed on the lake all that day, and when the sun began to go down, a family of raccoons waddled to shore. We watched as the mother and her three babies washed and ate their food.

The next morning we got up at five o'clock and, following directions given by our hosts, parked the car on an abandoned stretch of road overgrown with grass. We climbed a hill and found ourselves on a rocky bluff overlooking the lake. We sat quietly. Sure enough, just as our hosts had guaranteed, we heard a splash. Our eyes searched the lake. My husband pointed to a marshy spot close to shore. Two otters were skimming along the water. They dove and played for a few minutes before two kits joined them. The family frolicked in the water, playing what appeared to be a game of tag.

When their game was over, they began to dive into the water, time after time. When we left them, the largest otter, which I assumed was the father of the family, was lying on his back, cracking open clam shells. It was time for breakfast—not just for the otters but for us as well.

That afternoon we took a drive to Horseshoe Falls. I stood spellbound as the water cascaded into a large pool of what appeared to be crystal-clear water. Mist rose from the area where the falls pounded into the pool, enshrouding the nearby woods in a soft white veil.

That evening we sat on the knoll behind our cabin, overlooking the lake. Light fog rolled in. The night became chilly. Suddenly, we heard twigs snapping as something made its way through the underbrush about five hundred yards from our cabin. Thinking it might be a bear, we sat, paralyzed.

What we saw next was one of the most picturesque and beautiful sights I have ever seen. A bull moose lumbered out of the woods, down the hill and into the lake.

We watched him swim, holding his majestic rack of antlers high. Soon, to our disappointment, he disappeared into the fog. We saw many other marvelous sights that week, but this was the most profound—the most miraculous.

As I watched that moose, the doe and her fawns, and the other creatures in their natural habitat, I felt at one with nature and in tune with the universe. Even now, I often close my eyes and watch that moose swimming the lake. The sight has been forever etched in my memory. Each time I do this, as he disappears into the fog, my soul is at peace.

The Renegade Parrots

LONNIE HULL DUPONT

In San Francisco, a flock of wild green parrots lives near the Bay. Nobody knows for certain how they got there—after all, parrots are not native to northern California. One rumor is that a pet shop burned down and these parrots managed to save themselves and become a renegade flock. Whatever the reason, this flock has been living on Russian Hill and Telegraph Hill for many years, flying between the two hills, chattering for those lucky enough to see or hear them.

I lived on Telegraph Hill for many years, in the North Beach neighborhood of the city. During my first six years I heard about the parrots, but I never saw them. I'd heard of people seeing them, but I never talked to anyone who actually had. In fact, I had one friend who was convinced that the existence of the wild parrots in San Francisco was an urban myth.

In my fifth year in San Francisco, I got married. My husband and I stayed in my original apartment on the side of Telegraph Hill for the next few years. This was a golden time. We were true, dewy-eyed San Franciscans, in love with our quirky neighborhood, with the billowing fog that burned off by noon and with each other. We were in good health and crazy about life. We felt unbelievably blessed.

Each morning for exercise, I took walks up Telegraph Hill, one of the city's several steep hills where sometimes the very sidewalks are flights of stairs. At the top of Telegraph Hill, I'd watch the sun rise out of the Bay, illuminating the dozens of Chinese neighbors scattered around the hilltop doing group calisthenics or tai chi. I'd circle Coit Tower and then head back down the hill through a grove of bottlebrush trees and bushes of holly. At a short group of stairs, I would always stop, look around at the beauty and sigh with pure San Francisco pleasure. Then I'd descend the stairs and wind my way home.

One morning, I'd walked my walk, climbed the hill, nodded to some of the Chinese exercisers, and headed down through the grove to the stairs. As usual, I stopped at the top of the steps, looked out over the Bay and took a deep breath.

This morning, however, I prayed inside, saying how grateful I was for my life. I had had difficult years as a young adult, years full of stress and loneliness, punctuated with the untimely deaths of several people I loved. I felt God had been with me through all of that, and now I felt happier and healthier than I ever had. I felt as if, for now, I was coasting. I stood for a long time, letting the blessings of my life scroll through my mind. Then I looked up at the sky and said out loud, "Thank you, God."

When I started to take a step down the stairs, I suddenly heard such a racket overhead that I stopped short and looked up. There, surging up over the crest of the hill behind me, were the parrots.

I was stunned!

I watched the neon streaks of green against a dazzling blue sky and heard the screaming, squawking chatter of fifteen to twenty parrots in formation racing over me, heading west toward Russian Hill. I looked around quickly to see if anyone was around—I so wanted to share this moment. But there was nobody else. Later, my friend who didn't believe the parrots existed quizzed me in great detail as to what I saw. Yet she never did believe me.

But I saw them. I heard them. It took only seconds, and they flew directly over me immediately after I had thanked God out loud.

And, as that renegade flock of parrots became smaller in the sky, quieter, I heard the Voice inside that I've learned to trust over the years say loud and clear: *You're welcome.*

One Last Time

TERRI CASTILLO-CHAPIN

THOMAS CHAPIN WAS a hard-playing, spirited saxophonist-flutist who performed jazz on big outdoor stages and in concert halls and tiny clubs all over the world. He was an original who often said, "Music is my first love." The critics called him raucous because he played with such intense physical energy and prowess, sometimes "using yells, roars and howls to charge his performances." Yet when it came to animals, no one could be softer or gentler than he; furry and feathered creatures especially delighted him. They were, shall we say, his second love. So it is not surprising that, in 1997, when he suddenly fell ill at the age of thirty-nine, an animal—a black-and-white stray kitten named Moi— became a comfort and strength to him in his final days.

As a child in Manchester, Connecticut, Thomas had grown up around cats: Boots, an all-black cat with white paws; Felicia, a regal angora with a huge plume tail; and Thomas's favorite, Charlie, a plump, gray-and-white tiger (named after the legendary saxophonist Charlie Parker). Charlie slept at the foot of Thomas's bed during his teen years. I remember, when I first met Charlie at the home of Thomas's parents, how he had a strong and intelligent presence, an independent air. By that time, Thomas was living in New York City, pursuing a career in jazz, and we were dating. I was struck by how dear this cuddly creature was to him. Often when we arrived at his parents' house, the first thing Thomas did was rush inside, drop his bags, and call out, "Charlie! Charlie!" Thomas lit up when Charlie appeared. One year when we visited, his mother spoke softly upon our arrival. "Tom," she said, "Charlie was sick and had to be put away." Thomas's head dropped to his chest and, in silence, he walked to his bedroom and didn't come out until morning.

Shortly after, we were married and lived in a cozy one-bedroom apartment in Queens, New York. By then, Thomas had left a well-known big-band orchestra to form his own group, writing and performing his own compositions. He was happily making a dream come true. "I don't *want* to play, I *must* play," he said, explaining that music was his fate rather than a choice. Thomas was deeply spiritual, and he thanked God for the privilege of being able to do what he loved. Through the late eighties and nineties, he became widely known for his work in modern jazz with a trio that included a drummer and a bassist. Through his record label, he was regularly touring the United States, Canada, Europe and Japan, making records and gaining a following.

And animals? They were still a steady component of his life. Although our working schedules didn't allow us to have cats, we were able to have two perky, yellow cockatiels, Tweeter and Pai. Thomas taught them words and, by whistling, he imitated their irrepressible melodies and squawks. As for cats, they still surrounded him: in the streets, darting in and out of alleys, at rehearsal spaces, at friends' homes and on the road. He'd find them, play with them, and adopt them on the run. He even wrote and recorded tunes that captured the spirit of the animals he had known and loved.

Thomas was now busier than ever, at the top of his form. He was cited as "one of the few jazz musicians of his generation to exist in both the worlds of the downtown, experimentalist scene and mainstream jazz." Then, on one trip abroad, he unexpectedly fell ill. When he returned home, he was diagnosed with leukemia. This was stunning news, but even that could not keep him down. He brought that raucous playing spirit, along with his faith, to battle the disease. During his many months of undergoing chemotherapy, he inspired his doctors and nurses. He wanted to be back onstage playing, doing what he loved.

After three months of enduring some of the most punishing days a human being could suffer, he was in remission and returned home.

It was Good Friday. We both had so much to be thankful for; it was one of our happiest times. Although a long road still lay ahead, the doctors said, "Live your life. Play music." Between treatments, Thomas performed again in clubs and at outdoor summer concerts. At home, he read, listened to music and occasionally tried to compose, surrounded by the cockatiels, who cheered him and whose sounds and antics inspired in him fresh ideas.

Then at the end of summer, he received discouraging news. The leukemia was back and there was little more the doctors could do.

"I want to live. I want to grow old with you. I want

to play again," Thomas said to me. We mustered all of our energies and looked into alternative therapies and clinical trials. These were not the easiest of days, yet we had so much: our faith, our families and friends, each other. Thomas maintained a rigorous spirit and optimism. These days he wasn't playing music onstage; the instrument he now played was himself. His generosity, courage and humor were the notes coming out of him, and people—even strangers—were attracted to him. Often doctors and nurses called or stopped by the house to say hello, and former hospital roommates would phone him.

Between the new treatments and outpatient visits, Thomas spent most days in the sunny back room of our apartment—his music room—that overlooked a neighbor's small garden. We had to ask Thomas's father to come and take the cockatiels away until Thomas was better. His father took the birds to a children's museum near their home in Connecticut, where they were welcomed and cared for.

It was late fall and the days were shorter. The house was quiet without the birds. Treatments were continuing. Thomas was frail. One day I found him in the music room, sitting with the saxophone on his lap, tears in his eyes. "I just want to play again," he sighed. And then, as if knowing some truth that hadn't yet registered with me, he said, "I want to play one last time."

As the weeks passed, I began to feel the weight of the illness overtaking all of our long, hard efforts. I could see Thomas's fatigue; this was to be one of his most challenging periods. Yet he wouldn't give up. The desire to play music again fueled his fight. One day he stood at the window overlooking a neighbor's house. "Come quickly," he called. I ran over and stood next to him, looking out. He pointed to a small black-and-white kitten we'd never seen before frolicking in the garden. The energetic darling was making such a fuss, jumping high to catch a squirrel scampering up a tree trunk, darting between flower bushes, and having a . . . well . . . raucous time in the garden. Thomas was mesmerized, laughing at the entertainment. The next few mornings it was show time for the cat, and Thomas was the audience. Afterward, Thomas would return to his piano and play with renewed concentration.

One morning Thomas got dressed and said, "Let's go outside and find the kitten."

"I don't think so," I replied. "You know stray city cats aren't very friendly."

But Thomas was already out the door and I was trailing behind him. When he reached the neighbor's yard, the kitten—from nowhere—came bounding into his arms. Thomas just laughed as the kitten rubbed up against his face. It was as if these strangers were old friends.

Day after day, Thomas would go out to greet the kitten. One day he learned that our building superintendent had adopted the kitten and let her wander in the basement. That became the new rendezvous for Thomas and the kitten, now named Moi by our super's children. "We don't know where she came from," the kids said while feeding her milk.

The leaves started falling off the trees; Christmas and blustering snows came. Thomas was walking more slowly now, but having his friend in the basement somehow made things easier. Moi was becoming a special presence to both of us and we talked about keeping her ourselves. But life was too erratic now; we first had to get Thomas's health and strength back.

It was February; the snow lay packed under minus temperatures. A year had passed since Thomas fell ill. Musicians from his home state planned a benefit concert for him in his parents' hometown. For weeks the event was written about in the local papers and announced over the radio. By now Thomas had grown quite weak. "I want to attend the concert," he told me and the doctors. They weren't sure that being three hours away from them was a good idea. But on the day of the concert, the doctors agreed to let him go. Thomas, who had not been any- where in months, was overjoyed. A friend came to drive us. Before we left the apartment, Thomas tucked into his bag the silver flute his parents had given him for gradua- tion. He went downstairs to see Moi. She wiggled playfully under his embrace. "Good-bye, Moi," he said, hugging her close. "You be a good girl while I'm gone."

We left the concrete sidewalks and dense surround- ings of our city dwelling and breathed in the fresh, cool air and wide, open spaces of the approaching country. Arriving in the Connecticut neighborhood of his child- hood, Thomas perked up at the sight of the familiar scenery: snow-covered fields where he cross-country skied as a child, hills and woods full of tall trees, winding trails and icy brooks. He had hiked there often and found treas- ured solitude among the birds, the squirrels and the deer. When we arrived at his parents' house, he didn't go in immediately, but walked on the frozen ground and among the trees in the yard. He stopped and listened to the song of a bird. I think Thomas could have stood there forever.

We were in the kitchen sipping hot tea with his family when Thomas's father asked, "Would you like to see the cockatiels over at the children's museum?"

"Yes!" Thomas cried, and jumped up to get his jacket.

We drove over. It had been more than six months since we had seen the birds. When Thomas put his face to the cage, Tweeter and Pai began squawking and flapping their wings excitedly. They recognized him! He called out their names, gave his signature whistle, and they answered.

A little improvised concert was happening. The museum staff gathered around. We all laughed at the sweet scene. Thomas opened the cage and put his finger up to Pai; she jumped on. He brought her to his face and they played "nosey"—something they often had done. Meanwhile, Tweeter happily flew out and circled the room, singing. The reunion was enchanting and joyous. Before we left, Thomas spoke to the birds, giving them his gentlest good-bye.

That night, Thomas dressed in his favorite billowy white cotton shirt, jeans and boots. His parents drove us to the concert hall. The show had begun, and we were brought to the wing of the stage, where we watched the various bands perform and saw the audience. His parents and brother sat in the hall near the front. The auditorium was filled, with standing room only. We were touched by all of the wonderful music and heartfelt tributes. Meanwhile, rumors spread through the hall that Thomas might play. No one knew for sure, least of all myself. Then during intermission, Thomas—moved by all of the music and love he felt—said to his band members, "I want to play."

When the second half of the program started, they called Thomas to the microphone. As he slowly walked across the stage, the audience stood and applauded; many had tears in their eyes. Thomas too. Most had not seen Thomas for more than a year. He thanked everyone for their support and expressed his love. "I probably have breath for only ten minutes of good sound," he half-joked to the audience. Then he raised the flute to his lips; he played for a full twenty minutes. That giant spirit, which he had always been onstage, came to life. With overwhelming power, he played the most exquisite ballad, each note clear and articulated, a melody haunting and soaring. The tune was a favorite he had composed called "Aeolus (God of the Wind)." When it was over, everyone stood, breathless, clapping and crying. Thomas looked out as if he were memorizing every single face that was in the hall. Then he smiled, put his hands to his heart and took a bow.

At his parents' house, Thomas, although uplifted by the evening, was exhausted. It was late, but after a warm bath, I put him to bed. He slept comfortably. In the morning he awoke with a fever, and the next day he was admitted to the hospital. It was pneumonia. We both knew this was the end. "I'm at peace," he told me, "because of Sunday—." He meant the night of the concert when he had played one last time. We said what were to be our last "I love you's." Then Thomas was placed in intensive care and ten days later he passed on. He died doing what he loved and fulfilling his deepest wish to play. *Not because I want to play; because I must.*

⚮

Nine months after Thomas died, the building super came to the apartment to fix a bathroom pipe. He spoke of Thomas and how much he had liked him. He had seen Thomas perform once, he said, and had enjoyed it very much. As he was leaving, he paused in the doorway. "By the way, do you remember Moi, the kitten that lived in the basement?" he asked. "Well, right after Thomas died, she just disappeared."

Some days I imagine Thomas, over there, playing some raucous jazz, with Moi turning somersaults at his feet. Thomas is laughing, still doing what he loves.

SPECIAL
MESSENGERS

*"See that you do not look down
on one of these little ones. For I tell you
that their angels in heaven always
see the face of my Father in heaven."*

MATTHEW 18:10 (NIV)

A New Beginning

SARA JORDAN

SHE WAS A PITIFUL-LOOKING MUTT, leaning into her wire cage door at the animal shelter, straining for us to pet her through the mesh. She was silent, in contrast to all the animated barking of the other dogs in the neighboring kennels. She only looked at us imploringly with great big brown eyes. "Save me," she seemed to be saying. Mostly black Lab, partly unknown, she was frizzy and dirty, abandoned because she "pulled too hard" on the leash.

"She'll outgrow that," my husband Dave and I said to each other confidently. We didn't learn until much later that it was not merely a behavior characteristic of a barely year-old dog but sheer enthusiasm and strength of spirit that made her forever lunge forward on the leash. If one is lucky, these are qualities that should never be outgrown. Bear taught us that.

"Bear? That's a dumb name for a girl dog," we said. But she answered to it, nevertheless, the only remnant from an owner who had kept her less than a year and dumped her off with no more than an obligatory information card. So Bear she was and is. Come to think of it, it suits her well. She's black as coal, other than a dash of white on her chest and one front paw. She's all chops and paws and hind end and love.

"What's the red ribbon on her cage?" Dave asked the shelter attendant. We noticed she was one of a few dogs that had one on the cage door.

"Oh, that means she doesn't have much time left," the attendant answered while mopping the floor.

"What do you mean?" I asked, although I already knew that they could keep each dog only twenty-one days before they euthanized them. Bear's clock was ticking.

The attendant read the information card on Bear's cage. "Actually, this dog was supposed to be put down this morning. We've got somebody new working here, though, and he accidentally put her back in the cage after he cleaned it, so we figured we'd wait until tomorrow."

Tears came to my eyes. Death had come for Bear that day and she hadn't even realized her narrow escape. How could we not take her? Bear had borrowed time and kept the change. This was a dog that could teach us a lesson in the richness of life and its bald-faced fragility. This was a dog that had come face to face with the harsh realities of life and still pulled hard on the leash. She was ours.

The first order of business was a bath. Rivulets of dirt and dust poured from Bear in our bathtub that night. Afraid at first, she began to enjoy the bath and the feeling of being clean and cared for. Who would've known that underneath it all Bear had a thick, shiny coat of fur?

We put a collar on her and officially claimed her as our own. She seemed proud of her new status and really came alive. This dog that had been so quiet at the shelter found her voice quickly and often. We took her to the park, where she ran freely back and forth between us. Bear was a new dog, all right.

Six-and-a-half years later, we cannot imagine life without Bear. She sleeps on my feet now as I type, unaware that I am once again remembering her rocky start in life. She is also unaware of how essential her existence is to me in contemplating my own life. God brought us to the animal shelter that day by happenstance, to save a dog that should have died before we even saw her. God also sent His only Son, Jesus Christ, to save a world that was unaware of its precarious position on the edge of death. We are all dead in our sins, but through the salvation of Jesus we are washed clean, set free and given a new life for eternity. We become the new creations foretold in 2 Corinthians 5:17.

If we only strain against the leash of sin and open that door to Him, death will one day call and find us missing too. We will be absent from the body and present with the Lord. Thank God for allowing a U-turn of eternal proportions.

The Aquarium in Our Living Room

RUBY BAYAN

As FAR BACK AS I can remember, there had always been an aquarium on the built-in hardwood divider shelf that separated the dining room from the living room in our old house. The five-gallon aquarium fit snugly into the divider as if the shelf had been specifically built around it.

My earliest recollection of this aquarium was when I was too small to reach the top of the tank, and I would climb up the arm of the couch beside the shelf to take an active part in feeding our colorful swimming pets. Somehow, in my youth, I considered the aquarium a basic element in our house, and feeding the fish an integral part of our family's daily routine. On some weekends, I would watch my mother clean out the tank, meticulously re-landscape and redecorate the habitat, and restock the tank by bringing in the most colorful tropical fishes.

We had a backyard pond that had some wild guppies and exotic swordtails, and my mother would pick out the best ones to put in our living room aquarium. This was the life I was born into, so the aquarium and the tropical fish just seemed to belong in our regular scheme of things.

In our preschool years, my brother and I were constantly attracted to the tank, and, of course, naughty as we were, we'd drop anything and everything into it to see how the fish would react or just to find out how our innovative underwater decor would look. A few shiny marbles were okay, but my mother would sigh in exasperation when she had to rescue such items as the flashlight we thought would remain lit underwater, the alarm clock that looked art nouveau half-buried in the sand and, of course, the multicolored crayons.

Patiently, my mother would tell us why these items did not belong inside the aquarium. "They are harmful to the fish because they pollute the water and disturb the balance," she would say, trying her best to make our innocent minds comprehend.

Eventually we understood that we couldn't drop our stuff into the water, so my brother and I resorted to "interacting" with the fish instead. We would splash the water and tap the walls of the tank.

"No, kids, don't tap the glass, because the fishes feel the pounding in their ears!" my mother warned us, emphasizing that the fish could hear our voices through the water, and they got hurt when we tapped the glass. I didn't pay much attention to what my mother was actually saying then. But I soon realized that she had been teaching my brother and me our first lessons in being kind to animals.

Over the years, the family aquarium continued to evolve, and the various fish inhabitants came and went. But there was never a time when we didn't have a bustling community of fishes that my mother would lovingly attend to every single day.

It was only when I was about ready to move out of our old home to live in a place of my own that I took the time to ask my mother the question I had always wanted to ask her. "Mom, we've cared for dogs, cats, rabbits and hamsters, but none of them became a constant in our lives like these fishes in this aquarium. Why is that?"

My mother eagerly answered, "Fishes in an aquarium are probably the easiest pets to take care of. You don't have to house-train them, take them out for a walk or bring them to the groomers. They don't give you allergies, and they don't keep you up at night.

"Instead, a thriving community of fishes in an aquarium move about gracefully and give you soothing performances of astounding hues and colors and smooth and agile motions in a world of harmony and indescribable charm." I told her I wasn't sure I totally understood what she meant, but she was glad to explain further.

"The fishes are my escape when life gets a bit harsh and unbearable," she said. "I just sit and watch them and blend into their tranquility and balance. They help me relax."

My mother then uttered what may have completely influenced my perception of tropical fish for the rest of my life. She said, "Very soon you will start your own family and live your own life. Remember what I told you about the fishes: they will help you maintain your sanity. They will give you peace. Let them do this for you as they have done for me."

I understood. And I remembered.

The Bobcat

LYNN SEELY

THE SUMMER I WAS SEVENTEEN will always be remembered as the summer of the bobcat. I was on my own and looking for a job—any job. I noticed a flyer that advertised "Carnival help wanted. No experience needed."

As I followed the directions printed on the handbill, I reflected on my situation. The way I saw it, being fresh out of high school and almost broke did not leave me many choices. And my old car wasn't going to last much longer, either. I yearned to be a writer, yet I could not see how that would ever happen. College, my stepping-stone to realizing my goal, seemed an impossible fantasy. No— my dream was never going to happen, and the sooner I realized it, the better.

I arrived on the outskirts of town where the carnival was set up and in a few minutes was speaking with Gert, the owner. I asked if she still needed someone. She did. She asked if I could start immediately. I could. She hired me at once. The entire process had taken only a few minutes. She explained what my job would be as we walked around. It had not occurred to me to ask.

I was to sit in a booth for a few hours each night and sell tickets. All my meals were free, I had a trailer to sleep in, and I would be paid a little something each week.

That night the carnival seemed pleasant enough and I was relieved to be settled somewhere. Lively, foot-tapping music played everywhere. Aromas of cotton candy and other delicious things wafted through the air. Bright lights twinkled and created a festive illusion. Children squealed with delight as they twirled and tilted in giant tea cups or rode on the other carnival rides.

People who worked at the carnival were known as "carnies," and they seemed to be friendly, open folk, with one exception: Gert's husband. He seemed surly and I decided I'd stay as far away from him as possible.

The second day I was with the carnival I wandered over to the "Wild Dangerous Animals Exhibit" tent. Many

vividly painted posters near the entrance proclaimed that
wild creatures were inside. Curious, I decided to investigate. It was a sad sight: examples of once-living creatures
were stuffed and on exhibit. They were in various stages of
disintegration. Most were moth-eaten and covered in dust.
The largest was a black bear that stood in an unnatural
pose, waving a supposedly warm welcome to all who
entered. Beyond the bear were other stuffed animals, all
dilapidated. The tent had live exhibits too: a variety of
snakes, housed in dirty glass aquariums, were displayed on
long wooden tables. But it was what I saw at the very back
of the tent that riveted my attention.

In an old rusted cage no bigger than four feet wide
was a live animal. The handwritten scrawl above the
cage read "Rare Dwarf Lion," but it was, in fact, a bobcat.
Her cage was filthy. She had no water or food, and the
only bedding in the cage was moldy straw that she had
been forced to use to relieve herself in. The stench was
overpowering.

As I looked at the bobcat, I felt immediate kinship as
well as profound sorrow at her plight. To her, at our first
meeting, I was the enemy. She could not flee, although
every instinct compelled her to do just that. She shrank

back, exposed white fangs, and laid both ears flat. Unblinking hatred glared in her eyes.

I knew something about bobcats. My grandmother had rescued a very young bobcat back in 1920. She would reminisce about Bobbie, as she came to call him, and I would happily listen as she told me of his many antics and habits. Bobbie never saw the inside of a cage. Ultimately, he took his leave when he was ready. He returned to the Everglades—to live free and wild.

I had learned to have a deep respect and love for this much-misunderstood species. Through reading, I learned quite a lot about the bobcats that inhabited Florida, as well as their western cousins. Bobcats—if given the choice—could survive and even flourish if they were in the right habitat. Even those that had been hand-reared.

I began visiting the bobcat after everyone else was asleep. I told no one. From around 2:00 AM until the sun came up, I would visit with her; then I would sleep during the day. I decided to name the bobcat Millie.

On my nightly visits I would bring her food and water. Because I could not open the cage, I would shove bits of meat through the bars and pour the water into her dish with the help of a funnel. At first she shrank back and acted much as she had the first time I saw her. But as time wore on, she began to trust me. I'd talk to her and sometimes sing softly. And one glorious night, she came to the edge of her cage to greet me as soon as I entered the tent. Her little stumpy tail wagged back and forth slowly, a sign she was happy. From that night on, I knew we were friends.

Sometimes she would playfully shove her paw through the bars when I waved a string back and forth. At times it was hard for me to remember that she was a wild creature. She seemed gentle as a house cat during my visits. Perhaps this was partly because she was still a young bobcat.

One evening after I had been visiting her for a few hours, I heard someone approach the tent. I darted behind a stack of boxes and hid. Gert's husband stumbled in. He was drunk. He headed for Millie's cage and banged on it loudly. The tone of his voice left no doubt how much he disliked the little bobcat. I had to stifle the impulse to leap out and confront him.

I watched silently as he unlocked the cage and scraped out some of the soiled straw. He then shut the cage and hung the padlock on before he turned and staggered off. He had not given Millie any water or food, nor had he replaced her straw. Happily, he also had not locked the padlock.

I came back over to the cage and stared at the unlocked cage door. The idea to free Millie had been getting stronger each day, and before me was the chance to actually do it. It would mean that I would have to leave the carnival, which was not something I wanted to do. Still, I knew in my heart that it would be the right thing to do. It was time to take a chance—it was time to set Millie free.

I reached up and removed the padlock and then slowly swung the cage door open. Millie was watching me intently. I spoke softly to her, just as I had many times before, but this time I backed up while coaxing her to follow me.

I gently shook and wobbled my miniature flashlight. The pencil-thin fluttering shaft of dim light barely pierced the darkness in the tent, yet it was enough to entice Millie. Her eyes became large as she focused on the light. This was a new game as far as she was concerned. She jumped out of the cage and followed the beam, just like a house cat would chase a string while playing. I lifted the tent door up, slipped through, and Millie followed.

I tried to stay calm as we walked along. My flashlight

grew steadily dimmer, but Millie continued to follow it. She trusted me enough to be relaxed. This was going even better than I had hoped.

Suddenly Millie froze, her interest in the flashlight gone. She realized that she was free! She stared into my eyes for a moment and then looked off in the direction of the forest. Moonlight washed over the silent grasslands that separated Millie from the dark trees of freedom. Though I could not see them now, I knew that the mountains that rose behind the forest would be an ideal habitat for Millie.

Millie was free to go where she wanted to be—and she did. She started trotting toward the forest. I was thrilled that she was free, yet tears ran down my face as I watched her go. I would miss her. She disappeared into the darkness without a backward glance.

I couldn't help but stare at the last place I'd seen her. I stood there for the longest time. Then I had to go. I had to leave this place and this carnival.

Just as I started to turn, Millie appeared at the edge of the darkness. For a moment we stared at each other. I think it was her way of saying good-bye. Then she was gone again, for good. I knew I would never be the same, nor would I ever forget the little bobcat. I had never felt so good about anything I did. It was good to set things right. And it was right for Millie to be free.

When the sun came up that morning, I was miles away from the carnival. My attitude and views on everything were forever changed that day. I was no longer the same person I had been. I had given the gift of freedom to Millie, yet I had benefited as much as she did. She was proof that I could change things, that I could make a difference.

It was a lesson I would never forget.

I was close to thirty years old by the time I got around to college. One of my classes was a creative writing class. The first week we were asked to write about something important to us, an epiphany. I was pleased with my grade. The professor had written a large A right next to the title: "Millie."

Buckwheat, the Singing Dog

MARY ALICE BAUMGARDNER

It WAS OVER TWENTY YEARS AGO that a lovable, golden-haired mutt named Buckwheat came into our lives. A photograph had appeared in our local paper, featuring him as "Pet of the Week." We dashed over to the animal shelter and adopted him into our family, right in time for our oldest son Matthew's ninth birthday.

As we sang "Happy Birthday to Matthew," we discovered that Buckwheat had a special talent. He sang. Buckwheat didn't howl, as other dogs might. He sort of came down on the notes, intoning an "oooh" sound. He traveled up and down his range with that "oooh." He had a certain poise, almost spiritual, as he got involved in the song. More than just noise seemed to be coming from him.

While our three sons were in school, Buckwheat would curl up at my feet as I worked at my desk. He listened with benign tolerance to my classical music selections. But he had a passion for Pavarotti. He came to attention at the first strains of "Panis Angelicus." With his front paws crossed, he would tilt his head back— and totally drown out Luciano. I liked "Panis Angelicus" and preferred Pavarotti's rendition to Buckwheat's. But Buckwheat was so soulful, so intense, I would never silence him.

"O Holy Night" was on that same Pavarotti Christmas album. Buckwheat would quietly listen to the English version. Then, as soon as Pavarotti began in French with "Minuit Chrétiens," Buckwheat would accompany him. We never understood why this was. Someone tried to explain that perhaps Buckwheat didn't know the words in English.

We had a friend who was quite a skeptic. He was certain we were embellishing Buckwheat's musical ability. The first time Bill met Buckwheat, I went upstairs and turned on "Panis Angelicus." Buckwheat didn't let me down. Up the stairs he trotted, with Bill following. He positioned himself in front of the boom box in my studio, crossed his paws, tilted his head back . . . and sang with all his might. Bill was astonished. "You should put him on television," he advised us. "He's incredible!"

Buckwheat's musical interest wasn't limited to vocal pieces. Matthew loved playing the piano but detested piano lessons. How grateful he was when Buckwheat would join in during those sessions. The piano teacher, who came to our home, was not impressed with a canine accompanist, however, so I had to bribe Buckwheat into the kitchen with dog biscuits.

As the boys grew older, Buckwheat broadened his repertoire to include their guitar arrangements. He was selective in what he would perform, but he always had an appreciative audience. Everyone thought he should be on television. Were we doing him a disservice by not sharing his gift with humankind?

Buckwheat's big chance came during a summer when the local news was as dried up as the fields. I had been interviewed for the newspaper because I was coproducing a talent show for teens. Although he wasn't scheduled to perform, Buckwheat sat in on the interview. I happened to mention his unique ability to the reporter.

Of course, a reporter wouldn't want to miss a chance

to hear a singing dog. So, in my off-key voice, I lured Buckwheat on with his old standard, "Happy Birthday." He followed along quite well, drowning out my part of the duet.

Buckwheat impressed the reporter so much that he wrote a two-column article that appeared on the front page. Accompanying it was a large photograph of Buckwheat with my son Michael. Folks loved it. They were grateful to read about something besides the oppressive heat, and it was a very well-written piece.

Several days later a representative from a Martinsburg, West Virginia, television station phoned. Could Buckwheat and I appear on their talk show? I thought my sons would do a better job, but the station manager insisted on me.

My personal apprehension about appearing on television was diminished by my great concern as to how Buckwheat would respond. There was no guarantee how he would act under the lights. Suppose he barked, or worse yet, suppose he wouldn't do anything? I should have refused the offer, but the boys were high-fiving and jumping all over the place at the prospect of having Buckwheat on TV. I couldn't let everyone down just because of my misgivings. At least I had the presence of mind to insist that they tape a video of "the singing dog" before the live show . . . just in case.

My television interview went well. Buckwheat didn't bark at anyone. But Buckwheat proved himself to be a temperamental tenor and refused to sing. I was glad we had the video backup. Buckwheat's television career ended in Martinsburg.

However, our local radio station must have been hard up for programming. To this day, I still don't know where my brain was when I agreed to pick up the phone and go on the air with Buckwheat. I had no desire for the community to know how flat I could sing "Happy Birthday." But I sang—solo. Buckwheat refused to perform.

I couldn't understand why Buckwheat was so provincial. Why didn't he want to share his talent with the world? Why was he so uncooperative? My opinion of him flagged. I hadn't expected him to provide income for the family, but I thought he could have been more responsive. I was disappointed.

However, Buckwheat was a wonderful part of our family for fourteen years. One evening, several years after his death, John, the boys' guitar teacher, stopped by. We all gathered around the kitchen table, reminiscing. I mentioned that I never did understand why Buckwheat would sing only for us.

It was John who put things in a different perspective. John, who sought fame and fortune with his music . . . who worked menial jobs to have more time to polish his stage performance . . . John, who wanted more than anything to be a successful musician . . . it was John who understood.

John explained that there are many who have talent and who want to reach the top, to be a star, to bask in the adulation of others. But there are very few who, like Buckwheat, have a gift that they enjoy sharing only with the ones they truly love. They don't need the praise of the rest of the world.

I think John was right. Buckwheat didn't need the limelight. He was content to share his talent with his family and friends, down on the farm. And how blessed we were to have had a singing dog!

$\mathcal{H}$is Reason for Visiting

RUBY BAYAN

$\mathcal{M}$Y FRIEND AND I sat on the floor, leafing through a dusty stack of family albums. Mark wanted me to help him pick out a few interesting photos to scan and post on his new Web site. We went over the albums as if we were viewing stills of a home movie as each of his three kids came into the world and grew to be the young adults they are now. The snapshots of birthdays, graduations, travels and holiday festivities immortalized the memories of faces, places and occasions that Mark's family had encountered through the years.

The photos showed that the kids had been fond of dogs. Various breeds and sizes of dogs showed up in many pages of the albums. But what struck me, as I scrutinized the photos one by one, was a black-and-white long-haired cat that obviously became an important member of the family. He sat with the children on what must have been a memorable Halloween because he was dressed in a colorful clown costume and you could almost detect a smile between his whiskers.

"You had cats?" I asked casually.

"A cat. We had one cat. Harry."

Harry appeared in a couple of Christmas family photos, posing as elegantly as the rest of the family. He frolicked for the kids in several snapshots of them having fun in the backyard. He sneaked in just in time to join a group picture of the family opening presents beside the Christmas tree. And in one of the kids' albums, Harry actually had a dedicated section—a pictorial.

"Harry must've been special to Michelle. She has a pictorial of him here," I said. I became curious because I grew up with cats and I know the kind of impact they can have on people.

"Oh yes, Michelle was particularly fond of Harry. Well, all of us were. Let's take a break and I'll tell you how Harry came into our lives." Mark helped me off the floor and led me to the kitchen.

While waiting for the coffee to brew, Mark shared a remarkable story.

Their family had just relocated from across the country, and the transition was extremely tough, especially for the kids. Adjusting to new schools, starting new friendships and coping with each other's anxieties stressed everyone to the breaking point. Mark and his wife bickered over their new jobs and responsibilities, and the kids resented having to witness the growing animosity. They were all getting on each other's nerves. The family was falling apart.

Mark remembered that one Christmas Eve, when they were hardly on speaking terms, he had to coerce everyone to dress up and attend mass—to be together as a family, even for one day of the year.

After the mass, as they all quietly hopped into the van to drive home, a curious thing happened—a black-and-white stray cat hopped in too. They tried to shoo him away and coax him out of the van, but the cat had found himself a nice corner behind the back seats. Mark looked around to see if someone would come looking for a missing cat, but all the churchgoers were busy greeting one another and rushing home to celebrate Christmas Eve.

"Let's go, Dad! Let's just keep him. He wants to come home with us." It seemed like a long while since Mark had heard his three kids agree on something. He wasn't about to disappoint them, so he drove home. Excited, the children focused on their new friend. The cat's well-groomed longish fur inspired them to name him "Hairy," which later became "Harry."

Harry stayed with the family through the holiday season. For a stray, he looked relaxed, at home, and unmistakably an instant member of the family. He had a friendly and loving way with everyone, and everyone loved him back.

"We don't know who really owns him, or where his real home is, so if he suddenly disappears, don't be heartbroken, okay?" Mark warned his kids.

The kids took turns feeding Harry, cleaning out the litter and brushing his fur. They enjoyed sharing the responsibilities of taking care of their precious pet. Sometimes they'd toss a coin to see who would keep Harry in his or her room for the night. And because the kids got along better, Mark and his wife relaxed and sorted out their differences. Harry had actually brought the family together again.

"That's the story about Harry," Mark concluded, as we walked back to the pile of albums.

"Wait! That's it?" I wanted to know more. "So, how long did you have Harry?"

Mark smiled, "Ah, that's the mystery there. We found him—or should I say he found us—at the church on Christmas Eve. Three years later, also around Christmas time, he disappeared—just as mysteriously as he appeared in our lives. I guess when he had accomplished his mission with our family, he had to move on to help another."

"Is this for real?" I asked. I wasn't sure I wanted to believe him. Mark sat down on the floor among the photo albums and smiled.

"Oh yes, it's for real," he stressed, pointing at more pictures of Harry taking part in a lot of activities they enjoyed as a family.

"We will always be thankful for Harry's short visit. He came into our lives to bring our family back together. He's out there now, somewhere, bringing kids and parents together again. It may sound incredible, but, yes, it's for real."

A Quail of a Story

ART LIENHART

ONE DAY IN THE late summer of 1999 I was bush-hogging a six-acre pasture for a friend. I had completed several loops around the pasture when a male quail came out of the tall grass and stopped about twenty feet from the tractor. I immediately stopped the tractor and turned off the engine.

First I must tell you that I talk to animals as if they were part of the family, and sometimes you might be surprised at what they will do.

I knew what the quail was trying to tell me, and I began talking to him. I asked him several times to call the female out where I could see her so I wouldn't run over

her. Nothing happened, so I started the tractor and pro-
ceeded mowing the pasture in first gear and looking for
the female. After a few hundred feet, I increased speed.

I made two more loops around the pasture, and each
time I came back to that same spot, there was the male,
just standing there. Each time I turned off the engine and
talked to him, but the female never appeared. I knew she
was in the tall grass, so I mowed very slowly.

On the third loop, still moving slowly, I saw the
female at the edge of the tall grass. Immediately I stopped
and turned off the engine. Following behind the female
were fourteen small baby quail, the last four barely able to
maneuver through the grass. Then I started to talk to the
female. As I walked to the front of the tractor, I was looking in the tall grass for any babies that might be having
problems.

I was less than ten feet from the female when the
male appeared.

I started talking to both of them, telling them they
had a pretty family and to take care of the babies. The
whole time I was talking to them, they just stood there
looking at me as if they understood every word I said.
Then I went back to the tractor, started the engine, and

continued mowing the pasture. As I went by the family, they didn't move, knowing that I wouldn't harm them. When I completed the next loop, the family was nowhere to be found.

Four or five days later, I had to mow a different part of the same property. I was approaching a burn pile when I noticed the male and female quail and all fourteen babies next to the pile. I stopped the tractor and talked to them again, explaining that they were in the tractor's way. Again, they stood still and seemed to listen. Then they led the babies over to a safe place and I continued with the mowing.

Two weeks later, I was mowing the pasture again. For some reason I looked to the right, and less than twenty feet from the tractor were the male and female in flight, going as slowly as they could. About twenty feet behind them were the babies, all fourteen of them, in flight. They crossed over in front of me and landed in the corner of the pasture and waited for me.

I drove the tractor within fifteen feet of the family, and nobody moved. I talked to them and told them again that they had a pretty family and to take good care of the babies. The female turned around, went through the fence, followed by the babies, one and two at a time. When the last baby was through the fence, the male stood there for a few more seconds. Then he turned and went through the fence.

I have never seen more than two quail in flight at one time—yet here was a family of sixteen that survived the raising of a family and said "Thank you" with a fly-by.

Question: Do wild animals understand what you say or do? You be the judge.

IN TIME
OF DANGER

I will be with thee:
I will not fail thee,
nor forsake thee.

JOSHUA 1:5 (KJV)

The Gatekeeper

GAYLE TRENT

*H*AD YOU SEEN DUKE, it isn't likely you'd have called him an angel. In fact, not even I called him "angel." I called him "my baby."

Duke was a St. Bernard, a gift to me from my parents on my tenth birthday. I arrived home from school that day and was immediately sent to the garage. And there he was, quite an armful already, but I gleefully picked him up and buried my face in his neck.

Early on, I taught Duke to rub noses with me. This kept me from getting drooly dog kisses, and it was our own special way of showing affection. When Duke was relegated to a doghouse in the backyard, I'd slip outside to sing him to sleep at night. We had a special relationship. He was "my dog"; I was "his girl."

One summer night after Duke was fully grown, I went out to refill his water bowl. I retrieved the bowl and filled it at an outside spigot.

"There you go, baby," I said, putting the bowl on the ground in front of him. I hugged him around the neck, and he growled. Taken aback and more than a little hurt, I went to stand beside his house.

"You might growl at other people, mister," I said, as he was extremely protective of me and had been known to growl at others, "but you do not growl at me."

My lecture was silenced when Duke came to me, jumped up and placed a massive paw at either side of my waist. He emitted another low, menacing growl. I was unable to move, and my dog's behavior was beginning to frighten me. He was my best friend, my guardian. Was he going to turn on me now?

I noticed that his face was turned away from me and that he was staring toward the road that ran in front of our house. As I watched in the direction of Duke's gaze, I spotted a man emerge from the shadows and walk down the road. Duke held me against the side of his doghouse until the man was gone. When he was satisfied that there was no longer a threat, he touched his nose to mine and let me go. As he thirstily drank from his water bowl, I hugged him and thanked him for his continued protection.

Barney's Gift

LYNN SEELY

$\mathcal{S}$ARAH LOOKED OUT her kitchen window and sighed. Last night's snow lay in foot-deep marshmallow drifts. To some it was beautiful; to Sarah, snow was a hardship. Now the front steps and cement sidewalk would need attention.

Today was Christmas. Sarah saw it merely as one more bleak and lonely winter day. No Christmas tree peeked out the front window. No light winked a cheery greeting and no gaily wrapped presents were to be found in her home.

Her home had once housed a tumble of children and noise, but today it was silent, a stark reminder of what was no more. She had been a widow for many years, yet not one day passed without her missing him. And her only children, a son and daughter, were grown and lived far away. She was expecting a call from her daughter later that day. It would be nice to hear her voice, and she would have a chance to thank her for the thoughtful gift, a much-needed check.

Sarah's son was in the Navy. He had been away for months and was unable to call or send a gift. She had no idea when she would hear from him again. Perhaps he would be able to call her today, perhaps not. She had to admit that being so alone was difficult at times. Other than the phone call, there was no reason to expect today would be any different from any other. Yet it would be.

Sarah was not as steady on her feet as she used to be, and during the winter she worried about slipping on ice and falling. She tried to be careful and always made sure to sprinkle salt on her front steps when they needed it. Once the salt had melted through to the cement, she would make her way down and take care of the sidewalk. No longer able to manage a snow shovel, she used a sturdy broom to sweep or push the snow off of a narrow path to her mailbox. She had done so only three days ago, yet it would have to be done again. For a moment she considered waiting a few days before she undertook the task, especially because no mail would be coming today, but decided against it. If it snowed again tonight, it would be too deep for her to deal with.

Sarah grasped the small can filled with salt and headed for the front door. She winced—arthritis pain made even this simple chore difficult. Occasionally the pain seemed more than she could tolerate, yet this morning it was the ache of loneliness that caused her the most distress.

She opened the front door slightly and tossed salt on the top step. Within seconds she heard the familiar, faint crackle that indicated the salt was beginning to change ice and snow to slush.

Gingerly she eased her way outside. She reached into the can for another handful of salt to toss and in doing so lost her balance. Down she tumbled. She hit hard, and the next thing she knew she was lying flat on her back at the bottom of her steps. For a moment she lay stunned by the impact, the breath knocked out of her. After a moment, she attempted to get up, but her first effort caused such pain that she cried out loudly and stopped moving. A few more attempts to move left no doubt. She wasn't going anywhere. She was unable to get up or even crawl back into her home. Pain radiated down both her legs each time she tried to move. She began sobbing, more from alarm than pain. In fact, if she lay absolutely still, it wasn't that bad. But each time she attempted to move, the stabbing pain stopped her instantly.

How she wished she had worn her winter coat instead of this nightgown and heavy bathrobe. She had boots on, but bitterly regretted not following her plan to put a coat on just before she swept her walk. The bathrobe was already allowing the cold to penetrate, and she was powerless to get back inside her house.

She wondered if this was how she would die. Was she just going to freeze to death? And on this day, of all days? She had no near neighbors and no one was supposed to come by today. Still, fear compelled her to call out. For a long time she yelled for help. She called until she was weak and her voice was too hoarse to continue. Her front door was still slightly open and she could see safety and warmth waiting, just out of reach.

She began to succumb to the cold. It was enticing her to sleep. She decided to let go, to drift off; she was so very, very tired. That was what she would do: she'd sleep for a while and then wake up and try yelling again for help. She just wanted to rest now. She finally closed her eyes and gave in to the deadly desire to sleep.

Sarah tried to brush an annoying bug away. She just wanted to sleep. Her efforts to stop the annoying bug didn't seem to be working. Gradually she grew more aware and her eyes fluttered open. She found herself staring into big brown eyes. That startled her wide awake, though it took a few moments for her mind to process what she saw. It was no bug that had annoyed her and awakened her from her deadly slumber. It was the wet tongue of a scruffy-looking dog. When he realized she was awake, his tail started wagging vigorously. Then, with one great sigh, the dog lay down right on top of Sarah. At first, the weight of the dog made her want to shove him off, but soon she felt the warmth of his body bringing life back into her.

She had no idea where he had come from. Perhaps he had heard her calling for help. No matter how he had come to be there, she was glad for it.

Sarah noticed that he was wearing an old collar, and as she talked to the dog, she read the name tag: Barney. A shiver ran through her. Her late husband had been named

Barney. Strange—it was certainly a very strange coincidence. By the looks of him, the dog had not been taken care of. He was thin and his coat was matted with dirt.

Another hour passed and Barney refused to abandon her. Sarah was well aware that her front door was open and the dog could have simply walked inside to a warm house. Yet he chose to stay with her. She had never known a dog could be so brave. His presence kept her awake and hopeful. She talked to him about her life and how she would love to give him a good home. Barney would whine-bark back to her. It was as if he understood her.

She didn't know how much longer she could last like this. She was so cold except for her chest, where Barney was draped over her. She heard the telephone begin to ring in her house. Oh, if only she could reach it, but, of course, she couldn't. But Barney could! What if . . . ?

"Barney—go get the phone." She spoke quietly to the dog. It was absurd to think he would understand, much less actually follow her instructions, yet she felt her heart pound with expectation.

The dog looked at her, unsure what she meant.

"Barney," she said, as she pointed and looked toward the door, "go get the phone."

The dog turned toward the door and stared. The phone was ringing—Sarah knew he could hear it. He didn't move. She pleaded with him one last time and urgently told him to go get the phone.

He slowly got up, took two steps toward the door, and then turned around and looked at her, as if waiting to be sure he was doing the right thing. For the last time Sarah pleaded with Barney to get the phone. She knew it was foolish to believe he understood, yet something told her he did.

At last he trotted into the house and out of sight. She heard the phone ring one more time; then it fell silent.

Oh no! They had hung up. Barney reappeared and stood at the door, unsure what to do next. She called him back to her and thankfully he came. He could have stayed inside and yet he came back. "What a wonderful puppy you are," she said, and hugged him closer. "Poor thing, you tried, didn't you."

Sarah knew she didn't have much longer to live, not in this cold. The temperature had dropped and she knew she had been here for hours. She longed to sleep, but each time she closed her eyes, Barney would lick her face and whine. He was keeping her alive.

Suddenly Barney sat bolt upright and turned his head toward the road. Then she heard it—the sound of a car. It seemed to be coming closer and she tried to yell, but could not. Then a car door slammed and she heard, then saw, the officer. A few minutes later she was covered by a warm blanket. Things happened fast after that. Within twenty minutes she was inside an ambulance, on her way to the hospital. As she was loaded onto the gurney, she asked the officer to look after the dog; he agreed to keep Barney until she came home. The rest of the night was a blur. By morning her daughter was at her bedside, and it was then that Sarah found out how the officer came to be at her home.

Her daughter had called to wish her a Merry Christmas. She let the phone ring a long time and then the phone was answered, but all the daughter heard was a strange breathing sound. She was frantic with worry when nothing was said and imagined that her mother lay in the house, injured and unable to speak. She hung up and immediately phoned the police to check on her mother. It was incredible to learn that the dog had actually knocked the ringing phone off the coffee table. "Mom, I didn't even know you had a dog! It's amazing that he knocked that phone over! You know, he saved your life!"

Sarah nodded in agreement and explained that she had told the dog to go inside and get the phone. "Except for that, he never left my side. And, honey, there is something you should know. I never saw him before that day."

The next day Sarah asked her daughter to explain to the officer that Barney was not her dog but that she dearly wanted him. So if his owner wasn't found, Sarah would gladly give him a home.

One week later Sarah returned home, grateful that the disc in her spine, the reason for all the pain, had healed nicely. She was told to be careful when she lifted things. That first day back home she had only one thing on her mind. She wanted to see Barney again.

In the afternoon the police officer brought Barney back. The dog bounded up to her, dancing and wagging his tail. "The owners never claimed him, Sarah," the officer said, "so he belongs to you. He was quite a Christmas gift, I'd say."

Sarah thanked the officer before he left. It had been good of him to care for Barney, and it certainly showed. Barney had been fed well and washed. His long coat that had been matted and dirty was now shiny and soft. Sarah realized that she loved Barney. He had proven himself to be the bravest, most unselfish creature she had ever known. It still astounded her that he had not left her and gone inside a warm house.

And his name—she couldn't help but wonder at his name. Her husband Barney had loved dogs all his life, but after he died, Sarah had not wanted to take on that responsibility. That is, until the day she fell.

She would never be lonely again. The day she came home, Barney also found a home. Some of the mysteries about him would never be solved, but that didn't matter. After all, you don't ask questions about a gift. You just thank God for it.

Weela, a Community Hero

RUTH GORDON

IF YOU DROVE UP the road leading to the Watkins' ranch near Imperial Beach, California, in 1994, you would have been greeted by a remarkable dog named Weela, a sixty-five-pound female American pit bull terrier. Officially an American Staffordshire terrier, and sometimes known as a Yankee terrier, the pit bull's unfortunate reputation comes from the men who took advantage of the breed's rare courage by training them to be bloody, fighting tools for unscrupulous gamblers. Without such training, an American pit bull terrier is intelligent, easily trained, strongly attached to its owner and guardian of its owner's property. The American pit bull is often called "the most courageous animal ever born."

Weela was never taught to fight nor was she harshly disciplined, so her behavior contrasts sharply with the pit bull's stereotypic reputation for viciousness. Weela was brought up surrounded by an affectionate family who taught her basic obedience and good manners. She was allowed to examine her world of animals and humans without undue restraint. She lived as an ordinary loving and beloved family pet, but her life was anything but ordinary. It was as if Weela had her own destiny and reason for being from the start.

One of ten puppies abandoned and left to die in a back alley in Imperial Beach, California, Weela had a precarious start in life. A near tragedy was averted by a chance encounter. Good fortune came to these puppies when Lori Watkins, an animal lover, happened to go to town to do some errands the day after the puppies were abandoned. Lori parked her car and started her errands, walking several blocks, stopping at the drugstore, bakery and dry cleaners. As she walked past an alley, she heard some strange sounds. They were not very loud, but they sounded like the whimpering of an animal or animals in distress. After she finished her errands, she walked back to the alley. She entered the alley and walked slowly in the direction of the sound to investigate its source. Lori was astonished to find a litter of ten puppies, apparently abandoned by both the mother and the mother's owner. She later found out that the puppies' mother was a very young American pit bull terrier that had been bred too early. When the owner discovered that the young mother, almost a puppy herself, was inadequate for her job, the owner decided to get rid of the puppies.

Once Lori discovered the source of the strange sounds, she hurriedly carried her purchases back to her car and drove straight to the alley where the puppies were huddled together, crying for food and water. She gathered them up in an old car blanket, put them in a carton she had in the back seat, and drove them home to her ranch not far from the city.

When Lori arrived home with her unusual cargo, the whole Watkins family enthusiastically pitched in and planned how to help the newest additions to their family. They fed them, watered them, played with them, kept them warm, and gave them the love they so needed—the puppies had a family of human surrogate parents. It was not long before the puppies started to flourish and grow. From the very beginning, one of the pups, a female, took a shine to the Watkins' young son. She would not let him out of her sight. She slept with him and followed him everywhere he went. In truth, this little puppy, whom they named Weela, adopted the young boy by simply claiming him as hers.

As the puppies grew older and stronger, Lori found good homes for each of them—that is, all but one. Needless to say, Weela stayed on to live with the Watkins family. Finding these puppies in such a vulnerable state led to Lori's special interest in the spay/neutering program of the Humane Society.

Weela grew up to be a very happy sixty-five-pound adult dog. She loved to run loose on the ranch, visiting with the horses, cows and chickens. She was unafraid of all but one of the animals. The only animal that baffled Weela was the goat. She was always terrified of the goat. The family seems pretty certain that the goat never charged her. Perhaps she feared the goat because he always put his head down in a menacing way or because he had such a funny voice. No one knows. For whatever reason, Weela was very careful to stay out of the goat's way. Weela also had her favorite animals. Her most favorite was a potbellied pig who seemed equally happy to see Weela when she came dancing and sniffing around. They sometimes seemed to have serious conversations about life, and their lives in particular.

Weela also participated in all the activities of the human members of her family. She loved to swim and when the family went fishing, she was there. When the family went horseback riding up the nearby trails, Weela followed along. And when the family relaxed, she joined them on the couch, typical of most people's pets.

If Weela was such a typical pet, what made her different? In 1993, Weela became the Ken-L-Ration Dog Hero of the Year, the fortieth dog so honored since the awards began in 1954. She earned this award because of the extraordinary courage she exhibited during a California flood. Weela did not just perform one act of heroism as so many other winners had, nor was her heroism solely directed toward her owners. Weela went on countless missions to rescue both strangers and animals over a period of three months. During this time she is credited with saving thirty people, twenty-nine dogs, thirteen horses and one cat, all of whom most likely would have died during the large-scale winter flooding in Southern California.

In January 1993, heavy rains caused a dam to break, miles upstream on the Tijuana River. Normally a narrow, three-foot-wide river, the dam break caused wild raging waters to isolate both people and animals for almost three months. When the dam first broke through, Lori and Dan Watkins and Weela went to a neighbor's ranch to try to rescue their friend's twelve dogs. Together, they worked for six hours, battling heavy rains, strong currents and floating debris before they were able to reach the ranch to rescue the dogs. The Watkins were amazed at Weela's extraordinary ability to recognize quicksand, dangerous drop-offs and mud bogs. She worked diligently and never let up. She exhibited both the tenaciousness and the strength of her bulldog ancestors throughout the day. Lori Watkins said, "She was constantly willing to put herself in dangerous situations. She always took the lead except to circle back if someone needed help." Weela's instinctive judgments seemed to be accurate without exception. The Watkins attributed a great deal of their success in rescuing the neighbor's dogs to Weela's efforts.

During the next month, seventeen dogs and one cat were found to be stranded on an island. On several occasions, Weela swam to the island, each time pulling thirty to fifty pounds of dog food that had been loaded into a backpack harnessed to her back. This took enormous strength as well as courage. Weela continued to provide these animals with food until they were finally evacuated on Valentine's Day.

During the peak of the flood, thirteen horses became stranded on a large manure pile where they had sought refuge from the raging waters. The frightened animals were completely surrounded by flood waters. A rescue team used Weela to guide them through the rapidly flowing waters until all of the horses were finally brought to safe ground.

One day while Weela was returning from one of her food deliveries to stranded animals, she came upon a group of thirty people who were attempting to cross the floodwaters. Weela became very excited. She refused to let them cross where they were trying to do so. She barked continuously and kept running back and forth, literally herding them to another place where it was safe to cross. Unwittingly, these people had been trying to cross the river at a point where the water was deepest and ran particularly fast. Weela knew that this was a dangerous spot, so she led them upstream to shallower water where the group was finally able to cross to the other side safely.

After several months, the Tijuana River finally became narrow and calm again. Once the emergency was over, there was no longer a need for a rescue dog, so Weela went back home to the ranch full-time to enjoy life as before. However, her community heroism was recognized. As the Ken-L-Ration's fortieth award winner in their annual search for the most heroic dog in the nation, Weela received a certificate of merit; a silver-plated, engraved bowl; and a year's supply of Kibbles 'n Bits dog food. Surely, the people she diverted from disaster and the animals she fed when the waters were raging around them will not forget her. Weela's life seemed to have found its purpose and destiny. However, if you saw her today running around the ranch, you would think she was just a delightful but ordinary pet.

Kimberly's Best Friend

BRAD STEIGER

GREG HARDING DELIBERATED for days before he decided to buy a cat for his seven-year-old daughter. In March 1991 he had just reached the point where he could afford to move his family to a quiet suburb of Seattle, and he thought it would be nice if Kimberly had a pet.

But Harding had lost several cats when he was a boy. He would just begin to grow attached to them when they would either wander off and never return or would meet with fatal accidents on the street in front of their home in El Cajon, California. He had come to consider cats unstable, unreliable, perfidious creatures—that were also very accident prone.

When he brought home Elvira, a young black female, he had a little talk prepared to protect Kimberly's feelings. He told her that cats were more like visitors than permanent members of the family. Cats should be treated with love and respect, but one should never expect them to stay for very long. Kimberly should not be hurt or take it personally if Elvira just up and disappeared one day.

As the months went by and Elvira turned out to be a regular homebody and a wonderful friend to Kimberly, Harding began to wonder whether the jinx he had always experienced with cats had at last been broken.

"Elvira has brought Kimberly so much happiness," Karen Harding, Greg's wife, said to him one evening. "I'm so happy you were able to rise above your own childhood disappointment in cats."

On the night when Elvira failed to return home, Harding felt he might be guilty of some terrible self-fulfilling prophecy. He stood quietly at the door of Kimberly's bedroom as she asked in her evening prayers for Elvira please to come home to her.

Harding knew well the pain that his daughter felt, and a small voice in the back of his brain kept nagging, "I told you so. Cats never stay."

That night the temperature dropped, and although it seldom snowed heavily around Seattle, enough of the white stuff piled up on the ground to cause Kimberly additional concern for Elvira.

"Elvira will freeze to death, Daddy," she said, fighting back her tears the next afternoon when she came home from elementary school. "We have to go find her."

Harding knew locating a straying cat would be no small job in their area, which was still in the process of being transformed from farms and orchards to houses and yards. A number of rapidly deteriorating barns and outbuildings stood around the area. Elvira could be holed up in any of a hundred places—or she could have been killed by traffic, an unleashed dog or one of the raccoons that stubbornly hung on to their rapidly vanishing turf.

"Please, Daddy, we have to go out and look for Elvira!"

Karen saw to it that they were both well bundled against the cold, and father and daughter set out in the gathering darkness in search of their missing cat.

In spite of Harding's pessimism, after about five minutes of Kimberly's plaintive calling, they seemed to hear answering meows from an old, falling-down barn. Harding had to keep a firm grasp on his daughter's hand to stop her from running on ahead. He could not risk her stumbling over snow-covered debris or stepping on a rusty nail.

When the two of them finally found Elvira, it was hard to tell which of them was more amazed. The black cat had wrapped her furry self around the half-naked body of a very small baby girl.

"See, Daddy," Kimberly said, smiling through her tears of joy. "Elvira wasn't being naughty by staying out all night. She was taking care of the baby!"

The doctors at a nearby clinic agreed that the deathly pale baby would surely have frozen without the cat's constant attention. The abandoned child, only a few months old, had been kept alive by Elvira's body heat and by her vigorous licking. Thanks to the cat's intervention, "Baby Doe" would recover without any complications.

"Elvira is a hero, isn't she, Daddy?" Kimberly asked on the way home from the clinic, as she hugged the purring cat close. "She couldn't come home if she was going to save the baby girl's life!"

Harding agreed that Elvira must be forgiven for staying out all night without checking in. "Elvira is a hero," he repeated.

Private Smith's Joey

LYNN SEELY

$\mathcal{A}$LTHOUGH VISITING THE ELDERLY was still new to me, I had already discovered some nursing homes were a place of solace—and some were not. The nursing home I was en route to this morning had clean, bright rooms as well as a staff that was considerate and cheerful. Even so, the elderly inhabitants are quite aware they will never leave or live an independent life again. Depression and withdrawal are common—especially for the patients who end up forgotten by relatives who never bother to visit. Perhaps sadder still are the patients who have outlived all their loved ones.

After parking my car, I made my way to the nurse in charge. She was expecting me and had selected a patient who might benefit the most from a visit. "His name is Robert Smith and no one ever comes to visit him. Don't expect him to respond to you, though. He hasn't spoken in months." She smiled encouragingly as she added, "But he will know you are there and maybe that will cheer him up a bit."

A few minutes later I was in his room, seated only a few feet from the bed Mr. Smith occupied. I said nothing at first. After a few minutes I moved slightly, causing the wooden chair to creak rather loudly. Even then he made no sign he knew I was there. He had once been a strong young man, but now he was a pitifully frail old man who couldn't even walk unaided. As I looked at him, I wasn't thinking about how the years had produced this cruel transformation. Nor was I focusing on how sad it was that he never had visitors. My concentration was wholly on the dilemma of how to engage him in conversation. If I were successful in that, perhaps it would coax him out of his depression a bit. Perhaps it would lift his spirits for a little while.

I looked at his listless face. His eyes stared straight ahead, blank and lifeless, yet I sensed he had deep feelings coursing just beneath his mask of apathy. After a few minutes of uncomfortable silence, for some unfathomable reason, I blurted out, "Did you ever like dogs?" The odd question hung in the air, awkward and unanswered, for the longest time.

I was about to apologize and amend my question to something more normal, such as "Did you ever own a dog?" when I noticed tears forming in his eyes. A remarkable transformation was taking place in front of me. Slowly Robert turned his face toward me and stared at me, seeing me for the first time. His frail voice wavered as he spoke. "Well, I never did care for dogs much, at least not before that night." With that said, he paused. I had no idea what he meant, but just the fact that he had spoken to me was a good sign. I didn't want to ruin this breakthrough by saying the wrong thing, so I decided to wait and see if he wanted to comment further. As I waited, his shaking hand found the control panel to his bed and he pressed a button on it. It raised the head of his bed up a little so he could see me more easily.

Then he began a story, a story that took both of us to another time and place and introduced me to a remarkable dog named Joey. A dog, as it turned out, that had saved Robert's life during World War II.

Robert's face reflected deep emotions as he spoke. "It was the winter of 1944 during World War II, and I was serving overseas. I had seen my best friend killed when he stepped on a land mine. I watched the horror happen as if in slow motion. It was awful. Not too long after that, I was separated from my platoon, at least from what was left of them.

"I recall on this particular night I had made my way toward where they should have been, but when I got there I saw the enemy had occupied the area. Under cover of darkness I slipped away and made my way back to the only cover I could find—back to a house that had been bombed. It was all that was left that might provide cover for me.

"Soon after I reached it, I fell through the floor and down into what used to be the basement. I landed hard; the fall injured my leg and I suspected it was broken. I couldn't walk on it at all. I realized I was stranded behind the enemy line. It didn't look good at that point. Not good at all.

"I was only nineteen years old at the time, and it was easy to imagine I would not live to see twenty. I was all alone—and I had seen too much. Too many lives lost. Too much death. And now here I was, injured and in enemy territory, with little food and no way to stay warm. In that dark time, during that long night, I decided it might be easier to allow the cold to numb my mind and body and just quit. I was ready to give up.

"It's a hard thing to admit even now, but I didn't want to go on.

"As I lay there in the dark, I decided to say a little prayer. I spoke quietly, barely above a whisper, and I asked for help. Then I made my peace with God. That night, I didn't expect I'd see the sunrise the next morning. Just after I finished praying, I heard a noise. I didn't even want to breathe, I was so scared. My heart was pounding so loud I thought the enemy could hear it. It was eerie, waiting for the next moment, for the next noise. I suddenly realized something: I didn't want to die after all. Under any circumstances.

"Then I heard the noise again. It was closer. It sounded like someone walking toward me. I pulled my gun up and got ready to fire. Then it occurred to me that it was possible it might not be the enemy. Maybe it was another American."

Robert paused for a moment before he went on. "I took a deep breath and whispered, 'Who is it?'"

"Well, nothing happened for a moment and then I heard an answer. Sort of a whine or something. It sounded like a dog had answered me, and what struck me about it was that he had answered me as quietly as I had spoken.

"I snapped my fingers quietly, and the next thing I knew, a large dog was beside me. He lay down next to me after licking my face once. He seemed exhausted, and when I reached down to pet him, I realized he was extremely dirty. I could feel a collar around his neck and could tell he had a tag on it, but I couldn't risk striking a match to see what it said.

"Although I had never really cared much for dogs one way or another, I found it comforting to have the dog next to me. His body gave off a lot of warmth and I started feeling warmer for the first time in hours. We spent the night that way, next to each other. We made it through the long night together. I did see the sunrise that morning. At first light I was able to inspect the dog and read his tag. His name was Joey. He was a large dog, solid black in color. That morning we were able to look each other in the eye. His solemn gaze told me a lot. I had the feeling we had both lost friends recently. I said to him, 'Seems we're both in a mess, aren't we, boy?' Joey looked up at me and answered with a brief wave of his tail.

"Well, that day, and for the next few days, I could

hear the troops and enemy vehicles close by. At one point it occurred to me that I would be as good as dead if Joey barked at them. But he never did.

"The pain in my leg was pretty bad, but as long as I didn't move, it was tolerable. I had two major concerns. The first was that I might be discovered. I figured they would probably shoot me. The second problem was food and water. I only had a small amount of both."

Robert's eyes were bright as he continued. "Well, the first day Joey was with me, we just stayed put. But the next day, when I woke up at first light, I found out the dog was gone. I figured he had run off. And I sure couldn't blame him, though I missed him a lot. In fact, I missed him more than a lot. And I worried about him too. Well, just a few minutes after I woke up, I noticed something right next to me. An egg. Now that was a little strange. Had a chicken come up next to me and laid an egg? That was just too preposterous a notion, yet the egg was there. I picked it up and ate it.

"But not the shell. I didn't eat that," Robert clarified. "Anyway, just about that time, here comes Joey. Boy, was I glad to see him! Well, he walks right over to me and he lowers his head almost to the ground and he drops something—an egg! Then he looks up at me and waves his tail real slow. Like he was waiting for me to say something.

"Now I figure this is one smart dog, but even more than that, this is one very unselfish dog. I mean, here he was bringing food to me when he could have gobbled it all up himself."

Robert stopped talking for a moment as he reminisced about Joey. "You know," he began again, "that dog did that every day, just before dawn. Some days he would bring me one egg, and some days he would make several trips and bring me two or three eggs. And when I would offer one to him, he would refuse. I figured he must have been eating his eggs at the place where he was getting them, and then he'd carefully bring some back to me. He never did break any.

"Joey was successful at not getting caught and at preventing me from starving. He never deserted me. We stayed like that for almost two weeks. Right smack under the enemy's nose. And they never knew! I'd like to think that Joey was stealing the eggs from the enemy, but I don't see how he could have. He probably got them from some farm somewhere. No matter where he got them from, one thing for sure is that he saved my life."

Robert was smiling now, his face clearly communicating the pride he felt about Joey. "The allies finally pushed the enemy back and we were finally rescued. You know, I never did find out who Joey had belonged to. There wasn't any record of him anywhere. And I got to keep him. He returned with me to the States and lived a long, happy life with me. He was the smartest dog I ever saw. I mean, he had real intelligence. Joey lived with me over ten years before he died." Tears formed in Robert's eyes before he added, "But Joey had a legacy, you know. He fathered puppies with a dog that belonged to a good friend of mine. We each kept a pup from that litter. And Joey was great with that puppy too. He showed him the ropes and taught that puppy everything he could.

"I have a picture of Joey." With that, Robert pulled a tattered old photo from his shirt pocket and thrust it at me. I took it and looked into the face of a gentle giant of a dog. I smiled at Robert and then looked back at the photo. Joey looked just as I had pictured him in my mind. I returned the picture to Robert. He gazed at it for a moment and then carefully placed it in his pocket.

Robert fell quiet, yet it was a comfortable silence this time, a silence shared by two friends. I was so grateful that he had shown me Joey's picture and shared his inspiring story. I finally broke the silence and whispered one heartfelt word: "Thanks." As I spoke, Robert reached over, grabbed my hand and squeezed it gently for a moment. Then, with a contented sigh, he leaned back and closed his eyes. He was tired. It was time for me to go. I eased quietly out of my chair and tiptoed to the door. I was already looking forward to my next visit with him.

I could tell he was pleased that he had shared his story about his remarkable dog. And that in doing so, for a short time, he was able to be with his beloved Joey again.

When I returned the following week to visit Robert, I learned that he had passed away a few days earlier. The nurse told me that he died peacefully in his sleep. She turned to go, and then turned back to me and added, "You know, when Robert was found, he was clutching an old faded photo of a large black dog. There wasn't any writing on the photo, so we don't know any more about the picture. I suppose that may have been the last thing he saw before he went to sleep."

I didn't say anything to her that day. I would tell her what I knew about the picture another time when I was better composed and didn't have a lump in my throat. I left the nursing home, saddened by the news of Robert's death. Yet I did take a little comfort in the thought that perhaps—just perhaps—Robert Smith and his beloved Joey were together again.

COMFORT IN THE
HARD TIMES

*"When these things begin to take place,
stand up and lift up your heads . . . ."*

LUKE 21:28 (NIV)

Miracle Dog

CRYSTAL WARD KENT

KATIE WAS NOT a miracle dog in the television sense. She never pulled me from a burning building or fought off an intruder. She didn't wake me in the middle of the night because she sensed I was ill. She did none of those things, yet she saved me nonetheless.

In early 1987, my life was going along on its usual course. I had a job that kept me very busy and a fairly active social life. And because all my family lived close by, I saw them regularly—especially my younger sister Laurel.

Laurel and I were only two years apart and had always been close. We'd shared a room growing up, and in high school our circles of friends frequently overlapped, so there were many joint outings and parties. We even went to the same college, where again our social circles often intertwined. After college, Laurel and I still lived near each other, so staying in touch was easy. We talked daily and connected regularly for shopping expeditions, movies or the beach. We both fully expected to marry, settle near each other, and spend many years watching our children grow up together. In fact, we often joked about probably outliving our husbands and sharing an old house with a couple of cats.

Those dreams were abruptly shattered in March 1987. My sister and I were planning a trip to Florida in early May, the first big trip we had ever taken together. My job was stressful and I needed to get away; she was recovering from a broken relationship, and the idea of a trip to somewhere warm and fun appealed to us both. I still remember her phone call.

"What a trip we've got!" she laughed. "We've got to have new clothes! Let's go to the mall next Saturday." I teased her about her blind date that night, and we agreed to attend a basketball game that weekend. Then a work appointment arrived and I had to go. I didn't know then that it would be the last time I'd hear her voice.

Sometime that day, an insidious bacteria invaded my sister's system. It swam through her bloodstream and began attacking the tissues around her spinal cord and brain, and then her major organs. To my sister, it seemed like a bad case of the flu, but it wasn't. It was meningitis, and that night, while my sister hunkered down with blankets and ginger ale, hoping to feel better in the morning, the clock counting the hours of her life was ticking. Bacterial meningitis allows only a fourteen-hour window for possible successful treatment. That time had just about passed when Laurel went to the hospital the next day.

Initially, the emergency room staff thought Laurel had the flu. The symptoms fit, and numerous cases were going around. They gave her fluids and something to settle her stomach, and she began to feel better. In fact, my mother called from the hospital, saying they would be home around 11:00 AM. I went to do errands.

However, the hospital had done blood work as a precaution, and one physician was concerned with what he saw: a high white cell count. Laurel's blood pressure was also low. He ordered a spinal tap, but before it was completed, they knew. Laurel broke out in purple blotches, a telltale sign of meningitis. She was whisked to Intensive Care, but within the hour she lapsed into a coma. By nightfall, the doctors were preparing us for the worst.

I had started a prayer chain that afternoon. When I

initially visited my sister that evening, I was confident she would recover. She was far too young to die. It couldn't be happening, not to us. But as I stood in her room, clad in the required protective gear, I knew. I knew she was gone. Her heart was still beating, but her brain had long since left.

I took her hand, noting how small her hands were, much like a child's. I spoke to her but felt no connection. My Laurel, my sister, my best friend, was dead.

The next weeks and months were a blur. So many family and friends to tell, funeral preparations, her apartment to clean out, notices to send, and bills to pay. Our wonderful trip changed. I invited our friends to dinner and distributed mementos. I went back to work.

I tried to pull life back to normal, but I couldn't, and I knew it never would be. Then came that horrible first Easter, my dad's birthday, and then mine. It struck me how forever after there would never be anyone who got me the same kind of goofy gifts and cards that Laurel had, how I would never shop for her or see her seated across from me at family dinners. I remembered the red dress like mine that she loved.

I had bought it for her for Christmas, and it became the one she was buried in. I went to call her a thousand times a day to tell her some bit of news. I knew her apartment was rented and she was gone, but I could never bear to cross her number from my address book.

The flood of memories and "nevermores" was overwhelming. I wondered how I would go on. To my friends and family I was strong, but inside I was broken and lost.

By summer, my brother had met a special girl. We all knew Hazel was "the one," and her presence in Lance's life was helping him heal from Laurel's death. I longed for a relationship to heal me. When it came, it didn't take the form I expected.

It was a lovely summer evening. I had to go in to work especially early the next day and was getting ready for bed. My brother appeared at the foot of the stairs and called up to me. I was a bit annoyed at the interruption but went to the doorway. Lance stood in the shadowed stairwell, holding something; I wasn't sure what. I only knew he was grinning from ear to ear. I took a step down and saw the brightest puppy face I had ever seen. The dog beamed happiness, and the fat little body wriggled from head to toe as I approached.

"It's a puppy," my brother said, stating the obvious. "It's ours. We're going to call her Katie."

It had been many years since I'd had a puppy. It had

even been many years since I'd had a dog. My last dog had died some time before, and with work and school, I had yet to get another. This one was clearly a mixed breed. She was black with a white blaze and chest and four white paws. The tip of her bushy tail, which was thumping mightily, was white too. Bushy eyebrows adorned her face, giving her a particularly expressive look.

Lance and I sat right down and watched Katie amble back and forth between us. When she tried to run, she tumbled over after a few steps, rolled around, and then bounded up again. We both laughed and laughed.

That summer, Katie was my salvation. I spent hours petting and playing with her. We played toss-the-bucket and fought mightily over sticks and tug toys. She slept in my lap or by my side under a tree. The Fourth of July and other family celebrations passed with less pain because Katie was there with her merry face and playful antics. She breathed love and I drew it into all the empty places of my heart.

As Christmas approached, I felt a pang over not being able to shop for my sister as I had only the year before. I thought of the one less stocking hung by the stairs. But my pain was eased by Hazel's stocking joining ours, and Katie's. Katie was as excited as any child by the tree and the gifts being wrapped. She loved parties and this felt like a really big one! On Christmas Day, she stood by, quivering with anticipation as one by one we unwrapped our presents. Finally, it was her turn. Patiently she watched as we drew out a ball, a squeak toy and some treats. Then she went wild, grabbing toys, giving kisses, the tail thumping the entire time. To my surprise, I found myself laughing and having a good holiday. What could have been one of the darkest days of the year had been turned around by an eight-month-old dog.

As the New Year came, and the first anniversary of Laurel's death approached, we all were touched with sadness. But as March passed and spring bloomed, Katie's antics helped us recover once again. Soon it was her birthday, and no one enjoyed the day more. My mother gave her a large "gourmet" dog biscuit that Katie took almost reverently. She then carried it carefully over behind some shrubs and buried it. My mother was never sure if this meant it was a special gift and had to be saved for later, or if it was incredibly offensive in some way.

As those first hard years passed, Katie was my rock, my companion, my comforter. On days when the tears still fell, she licked them away. On days when I felt lonely, she was there with a tennis ball, plainly saying "Come and play. Let's have some fun!" And we did. On days when the road ahead seemed so very long, she was there, leading me off on a tramp. The walk would clear my mind and boost my spirits, because Katie always found plenty to explore along the way.

Katie reminded me that life is good and that we must always keep on living. She took joy in every simple thing: puddles, snow, piles of leaves, a flock of birds overhead, a good squirrel chase, a new tennis ball. When I looked at life from her perspective, I, too, could find joy each day. As time went by, those moments of joy increased, and I knew I was healing. My life would go on—without Laurel and our plans, yes—but it was still a good life and it was mine to live.

Katie also taught me about time. She always stopped to smell the flowers—and everything else—and she lived each day to its fullest. She sniffed the morning air as if she savored it, as if she'd never smelled anything quite that wondrous before. Some days she had me sniffing too. Occasionally, I'd catch a whiff of the sea amongst the odors of damp pine spills and meadow grass, and marvel that I'd never noticed it before. The way Katie lived reinforced the message of Laurel's death—never take tomorrow for granted. Take today and embrace all it has to offer, and especially embrace those you love.

From that summer on, I made sure that living was my first priority—not career, not social obligations, not chores, but time for my family, my friends and the beauty of the world around me.

Wings of Comfort

ANNE CULBREATH WATKINS

I HUDDLED MISERABLY in my porch chair, staring out across the rain-drenched fields. A few days earlier, a car accident had taken the life of someone I cared about. As if that wasn't bad enough, it had been raining for more than a week, and my soul felt as dreary and gray as the weeping sky.

From inside the house, the telephone shrilled a summons and I rose to answer it. As I spoke to the caller, I let my gaze wander around the room. To my surprise, I noticed a large black butterfly perched on the screen of one of the open windows.

Hoping not to frighten it away, I tiptoed quietly to

the window and studied my visitor. It was a beautiful specimen. There were powder-blue markings on the topsides of the broad, dark wings, and pale orange blotches on the undersides. Curiously, the butterfly uncurled its long proboscis to probe the fingertip I offered. When my phone call ended, I turned all my attention to the lovely creature.

"What are you doing here?" I whispered. The butterfly daintily explored the screen, placing its feet carefully at the edges of the tiny openings. It seemed in no hurry to leave, and indeed appeared to be taking notice of me. After what seemed like a long time, it fluttered its wings and lifted off. The papery rustle of those lovely wings sounded like music to me, and I realized that for a brief time, I had forgotten the ache in my soul. Then it came crashing back, like relentless waves on the ocean shore, and I returned to my chair on the porch.

A hummingbird feeder hung a few feet from where I sat, and busy hummers buzzed all around it. The rain hadn't dampened their spirits, and they squabbled noisily around the nectar ports. Normally I would be laughing in delight at their antics, but now I watched them through a haze of tears. Blurry little birds dipped and whirred, and I wondered if these tears would ever stop.

Abruptly, the phone rang again. I sighed and went to pick it up. It was my husband, and as we spoke, I stepped into the kitchen. Perched on one of the back window screens was another black butterfly!

It looked identical to the one I had seen before, right down to the ebony legs and the white dots that sprinkled its body. The butterfly strolled casually around the screen and then turned its face toward me.

"You're not going to believe this," I told my husband. "But there's been a big black butterfly circling the house and landing on the window screens of the rooms I'm in!"

Allen laughed. "Maybe it's following you."

"Maybe," I said. "Or maybe it's trying to tell me something."

"Could be," Allen agreed. We finished our conversation and I turned my attention back to the lovely winged creature watching me from the window screen.

I rested my forehead against the screen while the butterfly walked about. It seemed comfortable being so close to me, and even occasionally unfurled its delicate proboscis to touch my skin. Its presence was somehow reassuring, and I wondered again why it seemed to be following me from room to room. When it finally took flight, the same whispery rustle I had heard before sounded, and strangely, I felt comforted.

Rain pattered against the trees in back of the house and fell in long straight sheets to soak the front yard. I settled again in my favorite porch chair and watched as colorful butterflies danced around in the droplets. I didn't know that butterflies could fly in the rain, yet these were. Bright yellow wings flashed against the gray that colored the world, and I marveled at their determination.

A sudden whir of wings close to my head startled me and I ducked. The never-ending hummingbird battle raged on, regardless of the fact that I was in the midst of their battlefield, and I wondered how they kept from doing each other real harm. Then, to my amazement, the big black butterfly appeared.

It fluttered and floated, angling its way toward the hummingbird feeder. It ignored the fussy little birds that attempted to drive it away, and settled at one of the feeder ports. I could see it flicking its tongue against the port as it sipped the nectar. That was the first time I had noticed a butterfly at the feeder, and certainly the first time I had ever seen one eating there.

Just then, three hummingbirds perched at the other

ports and began to sip too. I was stunned. These tiny birds, who never even wanted to share the feeder with each other, were peacefully enjoying refreshment alongside the black butterfly. What I would have given to have a camera to capture this unbelievable thing that was happening right before my surprised eyes.

All too soon the meal ended and the hummers took to the air again. The butterfly lifted off, too, and drifted about on the shifting air currents. I held my breath as it slanted toward me, and then watched in delight as it deliberately perched next to my arm. In wonder, I reached out a fingertip and carefully touched the butterfly's silky body. It sat still and let me caress it for several seconds before it flitted away.

That black butterfly stayed on the porch with me until it was almost dark. I stared in awe as it danced and dipped and hovered in my space. Several times it landed on porch furniture near me, or on the wall behind my head. I watched the butterfly until it was nearly too dark to see. The last glimpse I had of my visitor was when it perched on the porch rail one last time. It dipped its wings in farewell before sailing off into the dusk.

It had been an amazing afternoon. One determined

black butterfly had accompanied me for hours. A butterfly and three hummingbirds had dined together, and I had witnessed butterflies dancing about in the rain. And although I still had plenty of grief to handle, for chunks of time on that rainy day my attention was diverted and my heartache soothed. My bruised and battered spirit had been lifted by lovely wings of comfort.

You Knew All Along

🐾

ANN VITALE

LYNN SLUMPED DOWN on the couch in the living room. What should have been a joyous visit to the hospital had ended in uncertainty and sadness. Her eldest daughter had given birth to Lynn's first grandchild that morning, but the little boy was jaundiced and had a fever. The doctors had no answers yet for Kenny's unexpected problems.

Thunder, Lynn's big male Newfoundland dog, padded quietly into the shadowed room and sat in front of her. He was sagacious and gentle, as a Newfoundland should be, and edged closer as Lynn sobbed for the young parents and their tiny son. She stroked the dog's soft fur and told him about her fears.

Thunder went to the basket that held his collection of stuffed and squeaky toys and rooted around until he found a softball, carried it over to Lynn, and dropped it in her lap. But instead of his usual woof and tail-wagging invitation to play, he sat down again, resting his massive head on the couch, his eyes on her face.

Afternoon darkened to evening, and still the distraught woman sat, sometimes crying, mostly just staring at the floor or talking softly to Thunder. From time to time the Newf would move the softball with his nose, tentatively swish the end of his tail on the floor, and lay his head in her lap.

"Goodness," she said at last, "Jim won't be home for hours, and I've forgotten your dinner, haven't I, big guy? And you didn't remind me."

Lynn went to the kitchen and measured out his food. The black dog proved he was hungry by licking up every crumb.

Lynn stood and watched him, but the light in the kitchen seemed too bright for her mood and she returned to her dark nest. She curled up on the couch and pulled an afghan close around her. Every nerve was on edge as she waited for a phone call with some news—any news. Her whole body felt chilled, as though her heart was shutting down with sadness.

Thunder reappeared, surveyed her for a moment, and then picked up the softball and again placed it in her lap, pushing it toward her with his nose. He waved his tail twice and lay down beside the couch.

Lynn spent the night in the living room, telling Jim she wanted to be ready if their daughter called. Thunder stayed, too, instead of opting for his bed in their room.

It was almost dawn when the phone rang. Their daughter had the doctor's reports. The infection causing the fever was already responding well to antibiotics and the jaundice had no particularly dangerous origin. Many babies had it, and a few days under special lights should take care of it. The intravenous lines would be removed then, too, and Kenny could probably come home in four or five days.

Thunder sat up, swooshing his tail like a windshield wiper on the carpet. He picked up the softball and dropped it in Lynn's lap again.

"Yes," she said. "There will be a little boy to play ball with you."

A Prince of a Dog

PHYLLIS HOBE

It WAS NOT a good time for me. My mother had died after a long battle with cancer. The company I had worked for was sold, and the new owners downsized all of us. Then my marriage came apart, and my husband and I made plans to sell our house and separate. Only one thing in my life was still there for me: my dog Trooper. He kept me going.

Trooper was a thirteen-year-old Welsh Terrier and I had had him since he was a pup. Originally I planned to enter him in dog shows because he was such a beautiful example of his breed, but he grew a little too tall and no longer fit the breed standards. No matter. I loved him dearly and he was devoted to me. He celebrated my joys and banished my sadnesses.

Like most terriers, Trooper was feisty and feared nothing. Although he got along well with other animals, he always let them know that he was in charge. I remember the time I took him to visit a friend who had a large German Shepherd. As we pulled into the driveway, we saw Scout, the Shepherd, standing in the yard, watching us. He didn't move as I parked the car and got out. Then I let Trooper out and he immediately took off toward Scout. Suddenly I realized what he was going to do. It didn't matter that Scout was three times Trooper's size; Trooper was going to knock him down. I had seen him do it before.

As he approached Scout at full speed, Trooper rolled himself into a moving ball, intending to hit Scout's legs and knock him over. But this time it didn't work. As the rolling furry missile came close, Scout simply stepped aside and let Trooper roll past. Fortunately, Scout was a good-natured animal and seemed willing to overlook the whole incident. But I have never seen a dog as embarrassed as Trooper was. When he came to a stop, he stood up, shook himself and ambled over to some shrubs as if Scout wasn't even there. Several minutes later, he came up to Scout in a friendly manner, as if he had just noticed him.

For most dogs, going to the veterinarian is an ordeal. Trooper took it in stride. In the waiting room, he climbed up on a chair next to me and took a nap while most of the other dogs were panting heavily.

He obviously felt comfortable with Dr. Gulliford, our vet, and lounged on the examining table while he got his shots. Just as obviously, Dr. Gulliford enjoyed the visit. "Trooper," he used to say, somewhat paraphrasing William Shakespeare when the examination and shots were finished, "you're a prince of a dog."

From the very beginning, Trooper approved of John, the man I eventually married. And the feeling was mutual, so that when I told John I would like to have Trooper present at our wedding, John agreed. In fact, John insisted we take Trooper along on our honeymoon, and the three of us had a wonderful time. After that, Trooper went everywhere with us, and if he wasn't accepted, we didn't go.

Now that John and I were going our separate ways, I knew he and Trooper would miss each other. I even considered giving him to John, but I just couldn't part with him. I needed him so much.

It was a hectic time. I was following up job leads and going on interviews and looking for a new place to live. And each time I came home I would hug Trooper with all my might and bury my face in his wiry fur. He stayed very close to me, and if I sat down he would climb up next to me, snuggle down, and rest his head in my lap. If I stayed long enough, he would fall asleep and snore so loudly I couldn't help but laugh.

Then I began to notice that something wasn't right. Trooper had never been ill, but all of a sudden he stopped eating. He was listless.

I thought perhaps he was missing John, but something told me it was much more than that. His powerful little body seemed to shrink, and by the second day he could barely stand. I took him to the vet immediately.

Dr. Gulliford was waiting for us when we arrived. He came out to the car, lifted Trooper from the passenger seat, and took him inside without a word. As I followed along behind them, I reached out to God and prayed. "Lord," I said, "I can't give him up now. He's all I have. Please let me have him a little longer—until I get my life together. But I don't want him to suffer!"

Tests showed that Trooper was very, very ill with a liver malfunction. He was going down fast, and Dr. Gulliford was doing everything he could to save him —intravenous fluids and medications of all kinds.

Dr. Gulliford even arranged to spend the night at the clinic. "But you go home," he told me. "You can't do anything here. We'll know in the morning whether he's going to make it. I'll call you."

I don't know how I got home that night because I was crying so hard I could hardly see the road ahead of me. And it was useless to try to sleep without my wonderful furry friend alongside me. I just kept praying.

The phone rang just before dawn. "He's going to live," Dr. Gulliford said.

"Oh, thank you!" I said, bursting into tears.

"No, don't thank me," Dr. Gulliford said. "I can't take credit for this. I've seen this illness before and I've never known a dog to live through it. But Trooper did. There's something—or someone—else at work here."

"I know," I said. "God answered my prayer."

When I went to bring Trooper home, Dr. Gulliford explained that he would need a special diet because his liver would never be normal and would not be able to process some substances. "For instance," he said, "let's hope he never requires surgery because his liver will never be able to handle the anesthesia."

Trooper looked so much better already, and on the

way home he enjoyed looking out the window. "Thank you, God," I prayed. "I'll take good care of him."

Over the next two years I gradually rebuilt my life. Trooper and I moved into a charming little house on an old estate where we had plenty of room for our long walks. I found a job on a newspaper and loved it. I made new friends, and we cared about each other. Through it all, Trooper's love strengthened me. As always, he was there for me.

When Trooper was fifteen, he began having problems. First he lost his hearing, but I had trained him with hand signals as a puppy, so I could still communicate with him. Then he lost his sight, and I knew that his time was up. Because he couldn't see or hear, he felt threatened by everything except me. I knew I couldn't be selfish. I had to let him go.

When I called Dr. Gulliford, all I could say was "It's time." He understood and said he would wait at the clinic for us.

I had one more thing to do before we left our house. "Thank you, dear Lord," I prayed, "for letting me have him a little longer." And in my heart I knew I would have him forever.

ℒonely Lady's Journey

CAROLYN PIPER

ℛAISING CHICKENS may seem an odd hobby, but for one reason or another I love them. In fact, a sand chair is a standard piece of equipment in my coop, for whenever I need time alone to think, recharge, mope or mourn some happening in life, I head out there and just sit quietly watching the flock.

One of the pleasures of spending time with them is that one learns to recognize distinct personalities within what was once a flock of indistinguishable animals. I have, for example, a rooster without a tail feather to his name who struts around as if he were the Sylvester Stallone of the feathered set. A second rooster, who is achingly beautiful and a full foot-and-a-half high, acts like Pee Wee Herman on the lam from the mob.

And I have Lonely Lady.

Lonely Lady has always been a bit strange. A Rhode Island Red, bred at a hatchery of gene stock that emphasizes laying eggs, no brains and no brooding ability, she was named by the children of the woman who gave her to me because she was a stark individualist in a flock of conformists. Contrary to her gene pool, she broods every spring, refuses to lay eggs until right before she sits down, and is a world-class escape artist of no small intelligence.

There are times during the year when, like it or not, I have to restrict the flock to their pen, because coons and foxes, coming out of a long winter with young to feed, start looking for a quick snack. For the most part the flock seems not to notice that they no longer have the run of the yard, but being the bull-headed individual that she is, Lonely Lady most certainly does notice and takes sharp exception to the situation.

For one thing, she misses the treats she gets when she wanders into the house to request peanut butter on her rice cake. For another, she is prone to taking long daily walks in the woods. So although I try to keep her in during the dangerous parts of the year, it rarely works. Make the fence higher and she tunnels under, fix the tunnel and she squeezes through somewhere else.

Eventually I gave up all hope of keeping her confined and grew resigned to knowing that each day, no matter what I did, she, and only she, would soon be out of the pen and on her way to visit the kitchen or off to parts unknown.

Then one late fall day she disappeared. Usually home by dusk, just in time to elbow the others out of the way when the nightly treat bucket arrived, this night she failed to appear. Nor did she return in the days that followed. I knew it was inevitable. You can't act like a three-hundred-pound gorilla, well able to cope with anything the world sends your way, if you are a chicken. Sooner or later you're going to end up on the wrong end of the food chain.

Time passed. Massive amounts of snow came in December. Temperatures dropped way below zero in January and February, followed by the promise of spring in the cold brisk air of March.

It was well into the forties one beautiful mid-March day when I decided to go for a walk. Idly running my eyes along the tree line as I approached the woods, I came to a dead stop, for there—shake my head though I might in disbelief—strolling out from among the trees, was a chicken. A very bald chicken—a chicken with no more than a dozen feathers—but a chicken nonetheless. A chicken, moreover, possessing an unmistakably familiar confidence of manner.

Lonely Lady, after five months of coping with Vermont in the winter with no shelter or food, was home from her walk. I stood there and watched her head for the coop. Her bare bottom looked like a bad imitation of a rubber chicken one finds in a novelty store. Questions raced through my mind: Where on earth had she been all this time? How on earth had she survived? One look at her told me she had not had an easy time of it. Quite frankly, she looked, and looks, dreadful, and there is a bit of a limp in her usual jaunty step.

But still, there she was. Against all odds. There she was: home from her walk; waiting at the coop door, impatiently glancing over her shoulder to make sure I was following to let her in.

Lonely Lady is recovering fast, but I am still adrift in awe and wonder at her accomplishment. Modern chickens are domestic animals, and Lonely Lady can no more fly to avoid danger than I can. Animal predators, snow, cold, lack of food—she beat them all. It is at times like this that the wonders and mysteries of life seem limitless, and I hold my breath in reverence at the resiliency and beauty of God's loving care that connects us all to one another.

Vera and the Mockingbirds

RENIE SZILAK BURGHARDT

I FIRST MET VERA IN 1983, when I moved to my little farm with the somewhat dilapidated farmhouse. Her forty acres adjoined my twenty-five acres, so she was my neighbor. Already in her upper seventies and a widow of ten years, Vera was one of those memorable women who live out their lives on their beloved homesteads.

"My Dwight passed on ten years ago," she told me on her first visit, when she came to greet me with a freshly baked peach pie and a welcoming smile. "And my two girls moved on to live their lives in cities, so I guess our farm will be sold to strangers after I'm gone."

"Oh, that's sad," I said.

"Yes, it is that. Our farm has been in the family since

the 1800s. It was Dwight's home place. We lived here since we were married, and raised our family on it, and I'm a-staying here until they carry me away and lay me down to rest next to Dwight in the little cemetery just a half-a-mile from here. Besides, if I moved, I'd miss my mockingbirds, and they'd miss me." I smiled at her remark, and as she got up to leave, I thanked her for the pie and the visit.

"Now you be sure to come by and visit with me too," she said. "I love company. When I'm not at church, I'm usually at home, piecing quilts or making dolls, and I'd love for you to see some of my work."

So the tall, thin, elderly lady with the soft brown eyes, white hair and warm smile became my friend. Soon I was over at her place regularly, watching her piece one of her beautiful quilts or work on her adorable soft, country dolls or just listening to her stories about life on the farm.

One late spring day, as we sat on her little porch chatting, a mockingbird flew out of a holly bush by the house. It landed on a nearby fence post and began singing its little heart out.

"I guess that's one of your mockingbirds," I said, as the bird finally stopped singing and flew close to the ground in pursuit of an insect.

"Yes, that's one of them," Vera nodded. "They have a

nest in the holly bush. They've been using it for several years now."

"How nice. And you think it's the same mocking-birds that nest there every year?"

"Yes, I do believe it's the same pair," she said. "See that platform feeder there, on one of the fence posts? Dwight put that up, years ago. That's where I place my treats for my mockingbirds. They especially love bits of fruit."

"You know, I always thought mockingbirds mainly imitate other birds. But they actually have their own song, don't they?"

"Oh yes! And a beautiful song it is," Vera said emphatically. "But they are very good mimics. One year, my Dwight actually taught a mockingbird to sing his favorite hymn, 'How Great Thou Art.'"

"You're making that up." I smiled as I said that.

"No, it's true. Dwight was a wonderful whistler. When he whistled, people stopped to listen. One day, after listening to a mockingbird's repertoire, he began to whistle that beautiful hymn as he worked around the yard. And he whistled it, and whistled it some more. A little later, I was sitting on this very porch, sewing one of my dolls, when I heard an unmistakable and beautiful rendition of

"How Great Thou Art" ringing from the boughs of my oak tree. A mockingbird had learned it from listening to Dwight whistling it." Tears welled in Vera's eyes as she recalled that special moment.

"Of course, one is not supposed to whistle hymns. But Dwight's whistling was so beautiful that I don't think the Lord could have taken offense at it," she added.

A few years later, I sold that little farm and moved twenty miles away to my present location. However, I kept in touch with Vera and still went to visit her regularly. One day, about five years later, she told me that she had been feeling pretty "tough" lately, and a checkup showed a spot on her liver.

"The doctor says they could operate on it, but more than likely it wouldn't give me much more time if they did. So I decided against it," she said. "As much as I hate the thought of leaving my mockingbirds, if the Lord is ready to take me, I'm ready to join Him and Dwight."

A couple of months later, one of Vera's daughters came and took her to Wichita with her, where she passed away shortly after, at age eighty-seven. Of course, they brought her back, and she was laid to rest next to Dwight in the little country cemetery, shaded by large oak trees.

Recently I drove back to my old neighborhood to visit a friend who had moved into the area. As I drove on Highway Z and passed Vera's old place, a sense of sadness and nostalgia enveloped me. Her little cottage was boarded up, her field was overgrown, the place looked unkempt. Someone from out of town owned the farm now; someone who didn't care how it looked. Suddenly I felt the urge to visit Vera one more time.

I turned unto the narrow dirt road leading to the little cemetery, just half-a-mile from Vera's home. I parked and walked to the largest of the large oaks, where Vera's and Dwight's graves were. As I stood there in silent contemplation, suddenly a beautiful song filled the silence around me. And, sure enough, it was a mockingbird, singing his heart out from that oak tree above the grave. I was awestruck!

Coincidence? Perhaps. But I walked away from there with goose bumps on my arms.

SAYING
GOOD-BYE

And God shall wipe away
all tears from their eyes....

REVELATION 21:4 (KJV)

The Cat Who Came Back

CAROL WALLACE

WE DIDN'T NEED another cat. When a friend dropped by with a tiny white kitten in search of a home, we determined to be adamant. No more cats.

This one looked around calmly, not at all intimidated by the two cats (one vastly pregnant) glaring at her from their separate corners. Then she yawned, climbed up onto my husband's lap and into the pouch of his hooded sweatshirt, and fell fast asleep.

It was love at first sight. We named her Olivia.

She was a skinny thing, with bright blue eyes. As I was accustomed to black cats, she seemed to me like the ghost of a cat—but far too lively to be anything but real.

She had a flair for satire.

We fed her what we thought was a generous quantity of food. She lapped it up and then tottered weakly to the kitchen carpet, making sure we were paying attention. She then threw herself onto her back, one paw flung limply over her forehead like some cinema tragedy queen, and mewed pitifully. We brought her more food.

My husband went to feed the dog. I heard laughter as he opened that fifty-pound bag, and he called me to come look. There was Olivia, reclining casually on the dog food pellets, taking a languid munch or two as the spirit moved her. It became one of her favorite resting places.

Once fed, she gave us an after-dinner show, a vigorous tail-chasing that we came to anticipate. A natural clown, she loved to provoke laughter. Even Peabody and Nell came to watch.

Olivia approached everyone and everything with ears up and forward—classic cat language for friendliness. She radiated love to everyone and everything without reserve, seeming to have no clue about the darker sides of life. Love and you will be loved was her motto. It worked.

Even the most curmudgeonly of creatures—my cat Nell—loved her back. I often came upon them: a fluffy bit of white sleeping soundly, with the paranoid and usually hostile Nell curled protectively around her.

When Peabody had her kittens under our bed, I peeked—and saw four tiny grey-and-black kittens and one larger white one suckling peacefully. Peabody only yawned.

More times than I can count, cat haters found themselves sitting and talking, unaware that they had been stroking a little white cat. Like a set of worry beads, she offered the comfort of repetitive stroking motions and soft, soothing sounds so unobtrusively that those receiving her therapy were not aware of it.

In the garden I was Olivia's shade tree. She also lingered beneath a small weeping Japanese maple that was just her size and that didn't keep moving as I did. She would inspect my work, make scary faces at birds using the feeder, and then nudge me in search of some quality time. She was my white shadow and furry clown, lightening the monotony of endless weeding.

That last day she stuck close to my side, taking brief side trips to greet the other cats, the wheelbarrow or anything else she could bestow some affection on. It was scorching, and we rested frequently, Olivia snuggled under the crook of my knee as if it were a parasol. The heat encouraged more resting than working—and so there was lots of quality time.

I'm glad.

Because the next day as I drove down the street on my way to class I saw something white and still through the rain pouring down my windshield, and I stopped.

She lay in a huge running puddle of water, almost as if asleep—except that one of her beautiful blue eyes had burst from its socket.

I forgot the car, forgot everything, and started up the hill with her in my arms, tears and rain mingling as I spoke to her—praying for even a sign of life, yet knowing it was futile. Olivia had bounded toward a car with love—but this time it didn't love her back.

I covered her with a scrap of velvet and waited for my husband. I wouldn't let him look—that eye hanging from its socket had traumatized me, robbed me of Olivia's beauty.

We buried her beneath her little Japanese maple, weeping harder than the skies. We couldn't eat that night, even speak much, except for the occasional angry word that fell from my husband's lips. I tried to remember the laughter our little clown-cat brought, but all I could see was that dangling eye.

Nell and Peabody declared a truce; they sat with me or prowled about, mewing, looking for their "little white thing." We huddled together until I heard a thump of frightening magnitude outside the window. Both cats' fur stood on end.

I wasn't surprised to see a cat shape in the window—all of mine thump on it if they want to come inside. But Nell and Peabody were with me—and the cat in the window was white.

I went closer. She looked at me, with eyes bright, blue—and perfect. Her bright pink collar still displayed its tiny antique silver cat charm. My mind denied it, but my eyes inspected every detail.

It was Olivia. A perfect, peaceful, beautiful Olivia.

She sat quietly, turning her head a bit so that I could see both eyes intact. I begged her to wait so I could open the door. If she had looked like a ghost cat to me in life, she seemed very much alive in that window. But when I opened the door, she was gone.

My husband was skeptical at first. But we knew that Olivia's role in our lives had been as clown and as comforter. And we needed comfort. So she came back for a moment, to show us that in that other world that few of us understand, she was whole and happy. Then she left for good.

But years later, her memory still brings smiles.

Tidings of Comfort

EVELYN BENCE

$\mathcal{L}$AST WEEK I DREAMED that for much of a workday a maned lion slept outside my home-office window, in the yard. Toward dinnertime, the lion awoke, stretched, walked and sniffed the grass. I went out, ventured a reach toward and then into the mane. While I was still petting, or after—I don't know—the Lassie-like lion disappeared into thin air, poof! Yet I continued to sense the friendly, powerful protection and later saw the lion peering out from under a picnic table, watchful but partially hidden.

The next morning, stepping into my writer's office, my spirit was unusually peaceful, sensing the presence and blessing of that silent lion, maybe the Lion of Judah or maybe Dollie, my chief childhood comforter.

My childhood was eased by two great comforts: my dog by day and my stuffed bunny by night. I don't remember receiving the rabbit; as far as I knew, he always was. Even now, the cotton bunny watches me sleep, sitting in a doll's highchair beside my bed. His black plastic eyes and pink nose have fared better than his cloth body. On some shameful day, Mother put him in the laundry and let him spin until all his innards coagulated in his extremities, there to lump forever.

And he now has a new friend who caught my eye several years ago at a consignment shop. It may have been Mother's last visit to my home in Virginia. As was often the case, she had no money on her. With uncharacteristic boldness, she did not ask but told Dad to lay down three dollars for a nonessential purchase; she had seen my wistful smile as I stroked the face and floppy ears of a furry white bunny with black plastic eyes and a pink nose. "Buy it for her," she said. He did.

So alongside his new friend, the silent night-watch bunny that slept with me as a child is with me, with me still.

But the flesh-and-blood collie dog, she is a different story. I clearly remember the afternoon she entered my life. Five years old, I was summoned to the grand archway between the living room and dining area. Being in on the secret, my five older siblings hung back. This was my moment, my gift, though I'm sure it was meant for all.

Through the kitchen, my dad walked in, a large cardboard box held tight between his potbelly and his thick hands. He set the box down in front of me, open side up, and there I stood nose to nose with a squirming, blonde, white-collared collie pup who licked my cheek.

Just thinking about that first greeting gives me goose bumps. I named her Dollie. It was the only day she was ever allowed in our parsonage house. Like the preceding family dogs, by Mother's decree she lived in the backyard or roamed the neighborhood except when confined because of winter cold or passionate heat; then we moved her into the small detached garage wedged between the frame house and the stucco church.

The older children had fed and combed and mourned a black cocker and a brown collie named Thistle. My father wanted a dog on the premises. For his kids to play with? Yes. To teach them responsibility? Yes. To ease his nostalgia for the animals "down home" on his father's Pennsylvania farm? Yes. To watch out for and protect his family? Yes. Yes.

In 1952, the winter I was born, Thistle's incessant barking in the garage woke the family at 2:00 AM. Smoke.

Flames. The garage was on fire and the back side of the house singed. If not for Thistle, the house would have burned, and who knows our family's fate. Thistle suffered a baseball-sized burn on her back, which Dad rubbed with salve that healed the sore but couldn't erase the wound.

Thistle survived the fire but not the winter. My older sisters have warm stories about the black cocker who eased their loss, but I hardly remember her. Once she jumped into my arms, I championed Dollie, looking as she did like heroic Thistle but even more like famed Lassie. It was a shame that Dollie never had pups, as she was such a mother, and not just to me. When my toddler brother Phil, playing in the yard, ventured toward the road, Dollie blocked him with her bulk and nudged him with her nose: Back where you belong, boy!

In time I was the one who drew her water and filled her tin-can bowl with a cupful of fragrant dog chow supplemented by table scraps and sometimes beef bones. In the spring I combed her clean of a winter's overgrowth. In family outdoor photos, she's at my side, my hand buried in her coat. Approaching adolescence, when I was sure my father and mother had forsaken their tenderness toward me, my dog was there to take me up.

In sixth grade, the year Kennedy was shot, the year I

was told we were moving away in the summer, the last year before my next-oldest sister left—like all the others before her—for college, Dollie was the friend who sat and listened. In July we moved to a farm; Dollie now had open access to a large barn, and any number of rodents had access to our house. For the first and only time in her life, Mother said we could have cats.

After a round of testy sniffs and spats, Dollie and the cat hung out like old blonde pals. But the cat's four kittens, nested in straw stored out in the barn, threw Dollie into a maternal crisis. Dollie, now ten years old, had never had pups; not to be denied this birthright, she claimed the kittens as hers. She licked them head to toe, nudged them to her dry belly, and carried them—the scruff of their necks clutched between her teeth—to her favorite bed. Then the cat would take them back. Then the dog. For several days you never quite knew where the kittens might be, nestled with whom.

And then it happened. We'd been away all day, and when we drove into the driveway, I sensed something was wrong. Dollie was in the yard, alone, sulking. The cat wasn't in sight. I went to the gray barn to find the kittens.

Two were dead, a third was dazed, and the fourth was

milking its mother. The conflicted mothers had obviously fought it out. And Dollie had lost.

Dollie never again went near the kittens. Nor did she ever recover the vigor of her youth. If dogs age seven life-years to our one, she was, by this time, seventy and slowing. Lame with arthritis, fat with lack of exercise, she slept most of the day in the shade of the picnic table out back. That summer, running my hand across her rump, I discovered open sores on her skin, which Dad cleaned and smeared with salve but never healed.

That summer we moved again, to a house with a small yard on a city street. And that summer Dad decided that Dollie wouldn't be happy in the city, that she should be put out of her misery, that she deserved a peaceful parting and burial in the pasture behind the barn. Dad negotiated this with us by buying a cinder-black cocker pup a few months before we moved.

I was sixteen when I hugged Dollie's neck and said good-bye. Cinder, the black cocker, eased my loss but never stole my heart. In a few years I went off to college, and Cinder was sent off to a country bachelor preacher who needed a companion to tell his troubles to.

I've never had another pet, always living in city

apartments with restrictions. Nor have Mom and Dad had a pet (children grown, responsibility taught), though the roster at my mother's nursing home includes Sadie, a long-haired mutt that Mother generally ignores. But one day this spring a nurse brought in a black cocker pup. To my sister's surprise, Mom grinned and with her good hand pulled the dog into her lap. Nose to nose, the squirming pup turned and licked her cheek. And Mother didn't pull away. For a moment she let herself delight in canine comfort, as I had as a child.

ॐ

Three months have passed since I wrote this story. And two months ago my mother died. Quickly. Peacefully. Since then I've thought often of the dreamed lion—or was it a collie who thought she was an overgrown cat?—who slept in the yard all day, let me run my hand through her hair, and peered out from under a picnic table.

I want to think that in her last days my mother, with uncharacteristic boldness, did not ask but told God to send me a comforter. By day. In the night.

Belated Gifts

TERESA OLIVE

SEVERAL YEARS AGO, our family rented a house that had a basement apartment under ours. The young couple who lived below us were quiet and unobtrusive. Their dog, however, was not. Cody was a typical black lab; a big, tail-thumping extrovert. He loved to greet us by planting his huge paws on our chest.

Our dog Tasha, an English Setter mix, was a kindred spirit. Because she shared the yard with Cody, they soon became fast friends. We often saw a blur of black and white fur as they raced neck and neck toward some hapless bird that had just landed in their territory.

The only time I saw any conflict between the two dogs was when we fed Tasha. Cody would bound up, expecting to share in Tasha's bounty. However, Tasha would bare her teeth and growl menacingly. Cody would change his strategy, dropping to his belly and inching slowly toward Tasha's dish. But this ingratiating behavior did not impress Tasha. The closer Cody got, the more Tasha snarled and snapped. Finally, Cody would slink away with his tail between his legs—until next mealtime, that is. Then Cody, ever the optimist, would replay the scene, with the same disappointing conclusion.

One day my husband Jeff came home visibly upset. He had just found Cody lying by the side of the road, killed by a speeding truck. Tasha sniffed at Cody's glossy black fur and whined.

Over the next few weeks, Tasha was listless, her tail drooping. She obviously missed her old friend. At the same time, Tasha's food dish disappeared. We replaced it with another, only to have that one vanish as well. There followed a steady succession of bowls, aluminum plates, even an old coffee can. They all disappeared.

Finally, the mystery was solved when our neighbor knocked on our door, her arms loaded with the missing dishes, some still half-full of dog food. "Are these yours?" she asked.

When Jeff and I nodded, she explained, "I saw Tasha headed toward the road, so I shooed her back. Then I noticed all these dishes in a pile."

Puzzled, I asked, "Where were they?"

"Well, you know," she answered thoughtfully, "it was right by the place where Cody died. Isn't that odd? Surely Tasha couldn't. . . ." Her voice trailed off in confusion.

Jeff and I exchanged glances. Could Tasha have been enticing her old friend back by offering him the one thing she withheld from him when he was alive? Even today, retelling the story gives me goose bumps. It raises questions about animals' intelligence and emotions. It also reminds me not to wait to show love to those around me. I need to share whatever blessings I've received with others—before it's too late.

The Summer of the Ham Sandwiches

DIANE M. CIARLONI

I DON'T REMEMBER how old I was before I realized a beagle wasn't the only breed of dog in the world. As far as I was concerned, he provided more than enough variety. After all, he was available in black-and-tan, black-and-white, tan-and-white, and black-tan-white. Not only did he offer a color selection, but also a choice of sizes: ten-inch, twelve-inch, fourteen-inch. What more could a person want?

Beagles are also extremely smart. Well, actually, wily might be a better word. Or, better yet, a combination of wily and smart. Their primary negative factor is that hound-dog bay that can drive a person crazy. Nose pointed skyward, mouth forming a tiny Cheerio-like circle, and a mournful sound coming from the throat. Sometimes they expend so much energy that their front feet actually raise off the ground slightly. Of course, there are times when beagles don't bay just for the fun of baying. Sometimes they do it because it's part of their job. Consider, as a wonderful example, Duke.

Duke was a twelve-inch beagle who knew how to do just about everything. I didn't believe in harming so much as one hair on any kind of animal. My brother, on the other hand, fancied himself a rabbit hunter. He was sixteen or seventeen at the time, which means I was somewhere in the vicinity of six. Now what could go better with a would-be rabbit hunter than a sure-nuff rabbit dog? Nothing. It was as natural a combination as ham 'n eggs or peas 'n carrots.

Very early one morning Fred took the .410 shotgun from the house and whistled for Duke. The duo headed for the woods behind our farm. Deciding to follow, I jumped out of bed and pulled on clothes. Once outside, I kept a respectful distance between myself and them. We passed into the woods and, almost immediately, Duke's nose went up. I'd never seen it wiggle quite so fast, but then, I'd never been rabbit hunting with him. My brother did whatever it is you do to have the gun ready to fire. Duke, looking for all the world like a person on a mission, moved solo deeper into the woods. No more than two or three minutes separated his departure and the beginning of a bay. My brother apparently knew this routine, because he hefted the gun to his shoulder as soon as he heard the sound. Momentarily, a cottontail cannon-balled from the woods, with Duke in hot pursuit. The beagle directed the rabbit smack in front of my brother.

Bam! The gun discharged. Bam! It discharged again. I was terrified for the rabbit, but when I looked, he was skittering back into the woods. Duke went in after him while my brother reloaded.

In no time at all Duke settled into another bay. The scene repeated itself. My brother lifted the gun. The rabbit came from the woods. Duke shoved him toward my brother. Bam! Bam! The rabbit charged back into the woods. And it happened a third time. Baying. Beagle and rabbit out of the woods. Bam! Bam! Rabbit back into the woods, but right there, the repetition stopped. Instead of returning to the woods after the rabbit, Duke turned and looked up at my brother. I'm sure he would have shaken his head if he'd known how, but instead, he turned on his heels and set out for home. In other words, enough was enough.

My father didn't believe in having animals in the house, so Duke had a huge fenced-in pen in the backyard. Of course, we lived on a farm, so it wasn't really a yard, because having a backyard was nothing less than a waste of productive land. Anyway, there was a large house in Duke's pen. It was kept well stocked with discarded blankets that, as soon as the weather turned warm, Duke promptly hauled from the house onto the front porch Daddy had built for him.

The wire surrounding the beagle's pen was made of three-inch open squares, more than large enough for Duke's paws. That dog learned how to scramble to the top of his house and then use the roof as a launching pad to propel himself to the fence. He landed with all four legs spread and immediately hooked his front paws through two of the holes. Then, with that support, he inserted his back paws into two lower holes. It was perfect. He could then scale the fence with greater ease than the most experienced mountain climber or agile trapeze artist. He reached the top, went over and somehow managed to "walk" down the other side until he was within comfortable jumping distance. He was then free to go about his beagle business.

As soon as we realized Duke's escape technique, we took measures to prevent it by installing a board at the top of the fence and all the way around the pen. Now the enclosure looked like Alcatraz. And Duke still fought his way to freedom.

The beagle escaped nearly every night. He didn't go anywhere other than the screened door to the screened porch attached to the back of our house. Again, using his multitalented paws, he opened the door and entered. The first thing he did was check Mama's old wringer-style washing machine. She sometimes put clothes in there in the evening, intending to wash them the next morning. If she had, Duke jumped in and made a comfortable bed. If not, he helped himself to the ratty sofa that provided Daddy a place to sit while he shed his dirty work shoes before going into the house. I don't think the washing machine or the sofa was any more comfortable than the pile of blankets in his house. I just think he wanted to be closer to his family in case we needed him during the dark.

There was a large factory across the road from our

house. It was originally built during World War II to produce munitions. I don't really remember what it did when I was a kid, but I do remember there were lots of workers.

Duke disappeared for a while every day, but we saw nothing alarming about that. You see, Duke was a confident beagle. He knew his way around the area. He knew how to hunt on his own (he certainly couldn't depend on my brother) and he knew how to escape his pen. His personality and demeanor were—well—a bit on the strange side. Truthfully, I think it was because he considered himself to be far more human than canine.

Everyone in the immediate region knew Duke. Many knew him by name and others by sight. It was a good thing, because the beagle harbored one extremely bad habit. That is, he didn't believe in walking along the side of the road. No. Instead, he walked smack down the middle. Many times we saw cars stop for him or move to the opposite side of the road to accommodate his passage. Try as we might, we couldn't teach him differently.

Anyway, back to the factory and the wily beagle's daily disappearances. His absences didn't fully settle on our conscious awareness level unless we happened to call him and he didn't answer. Otherwise, he was just gone until, one day, his timing and mine happened to coincide. I was outside and, just as I looked up, Duke was turning into the driveway. That was fine, but something was dangling from his mouth. It was . . . it was . . . a brown paper lunch bag. I removed it from his mouth (he didn't protest) and opened it. It contained a piece of cake and two ham sandwiches.

"Duke, where in the. . . ." Before I finished the question, a fellow in work coveralls came striding down the driveway, calling "Hey! Hey! Is that your dog?" *Oh no.*

"Yes, sir," I answered. Duke turned, positioned himself next to me, and sat against my legs.

I was definitely relieved when the man's mouth turned into a smile, a very small smile but still a smile. "He's been coming over to the factory for about a month now and stealing lunches. Sometimes he steals one, eats it on the spot, and then steals another one to take with him."

"But how does he get to them?" I asked. "Where do you leave them?"

"We have a small coatroom," he explained, "before you go into the main part of the factory. We leave our lunches there."

"How do you get into the room from the outside?" I asked. I felt as if I were reconstructing the scene of a crime.

"A screen door," he said.

The mystery was solved. There wasn't a screen door within five hundred miles that Duke couldn't handle.

"Did you look to see what kind of sandwich was in the bag?"

"Ham." He started laughing. "He never steals the bags with bologna in them. It's always the ham."

I held out the rescued bag. "Would you like to take this back to . . ."

I looked at the name written on the outside . . . "Sam?" Without waiting for an answer, I said, "I can try really hard to keep him at home."

The man shook his head. "Sam needs to take off a few pounds, so let the beagle keep the sandwich. As far as keeping him home, well, we're kind of used to seeing him. We'd probably miss him." Actually, Duke needed the same thing as Sam. Six weeks of ham sandwiches had added a few pounds to his twelve-inch frame.

It was Duke's bad habit of walking down the middle of the road that took him from us. He was six years old. It was a summer afternoon. He was returning from a visit to my cousin's house. And he was, of course, walking down the middle of the road. He was no more than a matter of feet from turning into the driveway when a car seemed to come from the proverbial nowhere. Duke didn't stand a chance. I was in the front yard with a baseball bat, watching the faithful beagle who thought he was a person make his way to his family. I saw the car hit him and I knew he was dead and, for the first time in my young life, I experienced two emotions. The first was gut-wrenching grief and the second was equally gut-wrenching rage.

There was no way the driver of the car couldn't have known what happened, yet he never slowed down. Brandishing my baseball bat over my head, I began running down the road as fast as my legs would carry me. "Come back here!" I screamed. "You killed my dog!" I ran until my legs were collapsing . . . until I could no longer see the green car . . . until I felt my brother grab me from the back and carry me home.

It was amazing how many people came by during the next week and offered their condolences. It was amazing because ours was a farming community and such grief over a dog wasn't one-hundred percent seemly. Then one day a group of coverall-clad guys from the factory knocked on our door. One handed me a brown paper bag. Inside was a picture of Duke. One of the men had captured him on film with a hefty ham sandwich hanging from his mouth. They'd blown it up and put it in a frame. I looked up to thank them, but the leader held up his hand.

"He was a good beagle," he said. "We'd give up all our lunches to have him back."

Yeah. He was a good beagle. I wasn't ten years old yet, but I knew that surviving this grief meant I'd be able to survive anything life sent my way. Not because I was so strong. Oh no, not at all. But, rather, because Duke would be right there to remind me of the "summer of the ham sandwiches."

Memorial Services

JOE McCABE

THROUGHOUT THE LATE eighties and all of the nineties, my wife Hilda and I lived on a farm in West Virginia. Our yard was approximately one-and-a-half acres and was bordered on all sides by meadows. A farmer rented the meadows, and he put a herd of cattle there to graze. He had four bulls and more than a hundred cows in his herd. Every spring almost every cow would produce one or two calves.

Hilda and I had a large organic garden, and we enjoyed working surrounded by the cows. Frequently, a cow would find a way through the three-strand barbed-wire fence that separated our yard from the meadows, so we became adept at herding cows to and through the gate that led from our yard into the east meadow.

One day during the spring calving season, we heard many cows calling in distress in the east meadow. A group of them were milling around on an upward sloping section several hundred yards from our gate. Eventually the cows moved north, and we noticed a large dark object on the ground where they had been. Hilda and I entered the meadow to investigate. As we drew closer, we realized that it was a cow lying on her side with her legs pointing uphill.

When we reached her, we saw that a calf was half out of her birth canal. Both the cow and the calf were dead. The mother had been trying to give birth uphill and had failed. This must have been her first calf. She was too inexperienced to know that giving birth downhill would have been easy, but giving birth uphill was impossible. None of her sisters had been able to turn her over and save her life.

We went home and phoned the bad news to the farmer. He sent one of his sons to check on the cow that day, but it took him several days to get a truck with a hoist to remove the bodies from the meadow.

That afternoon, around four-thirty, the biggest bull in the herd stood near the dead cow and called loudly.

Soon the whole herd assembled from all over the meadows; the other bulls and all the cows came and gathered around the dead mother and her calf.

Hilda and I watched with amazement. For nearly half an hour the whole herd stood facing the dead ones. Some of them made low sounds. No church congregation could have been more reverent than these cows were. Eventually they all wandered off to munch the grass of the meadow.

Hilda and I decided that we had witnessed a memorial service conducted by cows. We had never seen anything like it before.

The following morning, around eleven, we heard the big red bull calling again. And we watched as the whole herd again gathered as before, for approximately half an hour. That afternoon, again around four-thirty, the bull called the herd together. Every day at eleven and four-thirty the bull summoned them, and they came and stayed for half an hour.

After the truck came and removed the bodies from the meadow, the herd continued to assemble twice a day, every day, at the same place and times. This went on for nearly three weeks.

One afternoon Hilda and I realized that the cows had not conducted a memorial service that morning. There was none that afternoon. Nor ever again.

That was the only cow who died in the meadows while we lived on the farm. We were sorry for her and her calf and for the farmer, but we were grateful that we had been able to observe the memorial services the cows conducted for their sister and her calf. These services were in their way as wonderful and mysterious as any we ever attended for our dear departed human friends and relatives.

A Note from the Editors

GUIDEPOSTS, a nonprofit organization, touches millions of lives every day through products and services that inspire, encourage and uplift. Our magazines, books, prayer network and outreach programs help people connect their faith-filled values to their daily lives. To learn more, visit www.guideposts.com or www.guidepostsfoundation.org.